MW01093330

SHAME NO MORE

Dr. Richard Shaw

with Melody Farrell

THIS BOOK IS PUBLISHED BY LOST POET PRESS

www.shamenomore.com

www.lostpoetpress.com

ISBN: 978-1-944470-12-8

Lost Poet Press first edition paperback, July 2021

ENDORSEMENTS FOR
SHAME NO MORE

You may find your story in the chapters of *Shame No More*. I did. Through tears, and prayer, and joy, I found new freedom. And, I am better equipped to help others find theirs.

This book is the shining star at the pinnacle of Dr. Shaw's life-long pursuit of insight and wisdom about what plagues us most - shame. *Shame No More* distills his decades of study, teaching, research, pastoral care, and clinical practice, into an accessible and immediately applicable resource.

I only wish this book had been available during the years I worked primarily with pastors. I would have been more caring, empathetic, and helpful as they told their stories of shame and quiet pain.

Shame No More is on my short list of must reads.

Rev. Jared Roth Ed.D.
Co-Lead Pastor, Evergreen Christian Center
Co-Founder Sprout Digital
Ordained Minister in The Foursquare International Church

A cascade of words come to mind regarding this remarkable book: profoundly insightful, powerful, encouraging, deeply spiritual, and incredibly helpful. Richard Shaw writes with a rare combination of both grace and truth. I fist-pumped when I read, "grace transforms all our expressions of shame." So good. So true. I have made a list of people I plan on giving this book to soon. *Shame No More* is a must-read for anyone with a broken past—and that would be all of us.

Rev. Kurt W. Bubna
Senior Pastor, Eastpoint Church
Author of several books including
Uncommon Hope
Epic Grace: Chronicles of a Recovering Idiot
Perfectly Imperfect

Dr. Shaw has crafted an incredible resource we have all been waiting for! Shame is the leading cause of most, if not all unhealthy relational patterns and unwanted behaviors. *Shame No More* provides trusted words and practical steps for anyone who is ready to throw off every hindrance of shame and run the race set before them. Filled to the brim with incredible wisdom, Biblical insights, personal stories, and decades of clinical shame research, this is a must read for everyone!

Foundational to every relationship, *Shame No More* is a must read for every pastor, counselor, coach, and parent.

Terra A. Mattson, M.A. LMFT, LPC
Author of *Courageous* and co-author of *Shrinking The Integrity Gap*
Podcaster, Speaker, and Co-Founder of Living Wholehearted &

Richard has been known as the "Shaw Shame Redemption" counselor for many years, and what a blessing it is to finally see his life's work in print. Readers will be wooed by his humble, transparent story-telling style. Scholars will be impressed by the depth and breadth of research that has gone into this book. Ministers will be challenged by Richard's profound insights, as he prescribes "grace" as the antidote for shame. Illustrations of shame-based behaviors in this book run the gamut from forgetting the words to the national anthem in a public performance to cheating on one's spouse; so somewhere in these chapters we can all identify shame traps into which we have fallen. Dr. Shaw never leaves us in despair, as he prayerfully ends each chapter with words of hope and suggestions for healing grace gestures we can extend to ourselves and others. You have opened the cover...now, dig in and be blessed.

Stephen H. Allison, Ph.D.
Robert & Mary Ann Hall Endowed Chair of Psychology & Intercultural Studies
Professor of Psychology, Abilene Christian University

Richard Shaw's work and ministry have been so transformative! Shaw has finally put to paper what he has seen that works for decades. I am a thankful beneficiary. And so will you be! The ideas in *Shame No More* saved my life. And I couldn't commend them more to you.

Rev. A.J. Swoboda, Ph.D.
Assistant Professor of Bible, theology, and World Christianity at Bushnell University Author of several books including
After Doubt
Dusty Ones
Messy: God Likes It That Way

It doesn't take long for our lives to be filled with things that do not belong compared to the image of God in which we are created. "Shame No More" by my friend, Dr. Richard Shaw, approaches the shame caused from brokenness and the image of feeling "flawed" that many are drowning in and helps us all realize that we are to be full of other things. Namely, the things that Jesus is full of – Grace and Truth. (John 1:14) Dr. Shaw beautifully reminds us to be so focused on the reality of God's wonderful transformation so much so that his grace and truth fills us and then oozes from us in every relationship, including our relationship with self.

Rev. Jim Dunn, D.Min.
President, Oklahoma Wesleyan University
Former General Director of the Spiritual Formation Department of The Wesleyan Church
Executive Director of the Church Multiplication Division of The Wesleyan Church

Shame is often the ultimate damage inflicted on our identities. More than what it does to us, it is what we use it to do to ourselves. Dr. Richard Shaw shows us the tender mercy and the path of grace to free ourselves from this ruminating toxicity and to finally walk in the land of the living again. *Shame No More* is a rescue plan of forgiveness and wholeness for our souls.

Terry D. Hargrave, Ph.D.
The Evelyn and Frank Freed Professor of Marriage and Family Therapy
Fuller Theological Seminary
Nationally recognized for pioneering work with intergenerational families
Author of 14 books including
Restoration Therapy
Families and Forgiveness
The Essential Humility of Marriage

If you've ever failed, you need this book.
It might just save your life!
Dr. Shaw has written a powerful book about freedom and excitement and a whole new way of living! A way of living life abundantly.
We all have things in our past which we wish we could erase or do over. None of us have a perfect life. We've all done and said things which we don't approve of, or that others don't

approve of. The good news is that we don't need to be trapped by these embarrassing secrets or stories from our past.

Dr. Shaw takes our shame out of the darkness and into the magnificent light of grace. With the gentle hands of a pastor and the insight of a therapist, he guides us into hope and transformation. This is a practical and biblically-based guide to leaving the past behind (with all its shame and struggles) and embracing a future that holds all the adventure of a rich life.

Steve Stephens, Ph.D.
Renowned author and licensed psychologist
Written over 20 books with over a million copies sold, including
Rules and Tools for a Great Marriage
Lost in Translation
The Wounded Warrior
21 Surprisingly Simple Steps to a Great Life
Marriage: Experience the Best

Shame No More should be required reading for every boss, pastor, therapist, and life coach!

Shame sticks. It accuses, it condemns, and it destroys.

His humor and relatable stories will provide you with practical steps to grow from the pain of shame to a life of grace. This book will be required reading for my coaching clients.

Jay Puppo
Certified Productivity Coach
Small business owner for 20 years

Shame has been a plague of incalculable proportions since the very Garden of Eden and has continued to this day – and the only true answer is the knowledge and acceptance of God's grace. Reverend Dr. Richard Shaw knows this from his own research and experience. As a minister and professional counselor, Dr. Shaw has an understanding of shame and grace that is rivaled by few. *Shame No More* is a book that is both theologically deep and psychologically sound. This book serves as a refreshing well for the thirsty and belongs on the shelves of pastoral counselors and experienced mental health professionals.

Daniel Sweeney, PhD, LMFT, LPC
Professor of Counseling and Clinical Director, George Fox University
International Speaker and author on issues of child therapy, trauma, and parenting
Director and Founder of the Northwest Center for Play Therapy Studies

Defining shame eludes many, but experiencing shame befalls most. Dr. Richard Shaw engages the reader to not only understand the meaning of shame, but then to learn to walk in a place of grace and forgiveness that leads to understanding relational dynamics and turns destructive patterns of coping into glorious and powerful connections.

Sharon Hargrave, LMFT
Founder RelateStrong
Pepperdine University and Fuller Theological Seminary
Executive Director of The Boone Center for the Family, Pepperdine University

If you want to understand the nature and impact of shame on your life and relationships, the tools to escape that shame, and the insights to help you move into freedom and grace, then *Shame No More* is just the right book for you.

Through personal stories and professional examples, Dr. Richard Shaw shows us common ways we can get caught in a shame trap but also provides tools to escape the unhealthy patterns shame can foster. Through healing, rest, and forgiveness, Rich shows all of us how we can grow into a life full of freedom, joy, and grace. *Shame No More* is a wonderful book for personal and relational development. It is also an excellent resource for counselors, clergy, and anyone in a caring profession.

Rev. Russ Gunsalus, M.Div., Ph.D. Candidate
Executive Director of Education and Clergy Development, The Wesleyan Church
Ordained Minister, The Wesleyan Church

As a pastor, I have often seen how the calling to serve God can easily become driven by a deep dysfunction of shame. In effect, it's the human need to be good enough for God's acceptance and approval. I can tell you, it has been a big part of my own personal journey. My friend, Dr Richard Shaw, has helped me discover the life truth that we simply cannot be good enough, we can only be in love enough. This is the transforming power of God's grace.

Dr. Shaw is a world class professor and counselor. He combines an impressive equilibrium of head and heart perhaps better than any person I have met. He is an intellectual with gifted insight while at the same time expressing a deep compassion for all people. In his excellent book, *Shame No More*, Dr. Shaw's unique gift will take you on a journey of discovery. You will gain insight into the shame that we all carry due to our common human condition. You will also discover the profound compassion of grace that can transform your life – and any life – and guide you into a new and authentic way of freedom and hope. My prayer is that you will embark on your own personal journey with Dr Shaw. May the principles in his book, and the power of God's grace, liberate you into a renewed life of "shame no more!"

Rev. Kip Jacob
Lead Pastor, South Lake Foursquare Church, West Linn, OR

Licensed minister, Foursquare International Church

Documentary Film Producer, *Undivided*

A "must read" for those looking to emerge from the guilt and fear of shame. Shame touches so many parts of society and holds people back from reaching their full potential. I'm deeply thankful Dr. Shaw has tackled the topic and feel that this will be a tool for readers to reach new potentials in their lives.

Jordan Kent, B.S.

Former NFL player and NBA broadcaster

As someone who swims deeply in Honor/Shame cultures and who lives in systems enmeshed with shame filled scenarios, *Shame No More* is a powerful book to read. Dr. Shaw reveals through real life stories, solid research, and faithful Biblical paradigms how to see and deal with shame in our lives. I encourage you to immerse yourself in this rich resource. I'm sure it will help you!

Rev. Joseph W. Handley, Jr., Ph.D.

President, Asian Access

For my wife, Karen

To my children, Taylor, Madison, & Parker

In honor of my parents, Larry & Jan

TABLE OF CONTENTS

INTRODUCTION

As fate would have it, I wrote this book in 2020. Do you remember 2020? One of the strangest years ever! And on top of whatever strangeness you had going on in your life and world, I had a couple extra things going on in mine.

I happened to be on sabbatical from the university that year. My daughter was *supposed* to get married in Hawaii – that didn't happen, and we had to go to plan B which turned out to be a beautiful wedding in Oregon. My son was *supposed* to play his senior year of college football, which of course got postponed and changed completely.

Alongside all of those things that didn't go according to plan, in the summer of 2020, I received a diagnosis of prostate cancer. That certainly wasn't *supposed* to happen! First off, I'm not old enough to get that diagnosis! I wasn't ready to have urologists and oncologists in my contact list. It threw me off of all my sabbatical plans and into a whole world of medical treatments. It wasn't what I wanted, it wasn't what I planned, but it was reality. Thank God, I'm doing very well, but it was a strange and challenging year.

So here I am, writing a book on shame and grace, and here's what I want to say to you: whatever you are going through right now – if you're going through a train wreck of a year like 2020, or if you're going through the best year ever – I just want you to know that God truly loves you. His grace is more than enough for whatever shame you are trying to overcome.

In the church, there are lots of silent, hurting people. They don't know how to talk about their brokenness. They don't know what it is, or if it's okay to talk about it, or where to go for help. This brokenness can be defined by one, singular word: SHAME. Our churches are filled with people who are bound by their shame, living in a narrative that says they will never be good enough to earn the love of God. They are trapped in the idea that they must keep trying, keep striving, keep pretending to be clean and pure so that no one will see their true worthlessness.

How can the church offer hope to hurting people and be a place where grace abounds?

My prayer is that this book will be a starting place to begin to change this narrative. Shame is never what God intended for our narrative to be. He longs for us to thrive in the freedom of his grace.

A Little More About Me

We are about to embark on a journey together that is going to be pretty intimate. We're going to be looking into places in our lives and hearts where shame has held us captive, and then we are going to talk about how grace can set us free. I suppose before we go to those places together, it would be good for you to know a little more about me.

I was raised in a small town called Naponee, Nebraska. It's so small that people 60 miles away don't even know it exists. The population is right around 160 people – and shrinking! In fact, my kids won't even let me call it a town; they tell me I have to call it a neighborhood. My dad was a preacher for over 30 years, and a farmer for his whole life. The farm life was never a great fit for me, and school came pretty easy, at least early on. So, education quickly became the track for my life. I went to college, got a couple of master's degrees, became an ordained minister in the Foursquare church, and did a doctorate in marriage and family therapy.

In the 1990's, I wrote my doctoral dissertation on shame and grace. This path of study led me to begin a journey that I never could have expected: a journey of personal healing, the discovery of grace, and a calling to share it with all who would listen.

I love my family of origin. But they were not perfect. Just like I am not perfect. Just like you and your family are not perfect. Shame became the language that helped me make sense of some of the thoughts, feelings, and experiences I had growing up. I believed I had a lens on life that was working for me, but I was broken. As I began my research into the concepts of shame and grace, I began to experience personal transformation. For the first time, I could understand my life and experiences through a lens other than shame. I could work through my brokenness because I had language for my brokenness. I could move towards healing because I had language for my healing. The constructs of shame and grace fit; they made sense to me, and they began making sense for other people around me.

I have dedicated my life to this work around shame and grace, especially as it impacts the Christian Church community. I have studied the topic of integration of faith and psychology for over 30 years. For almost 30 years, I have taught a course entitled *Shame and Grace,* where I attempt to help future counselor educators engage in their own reflective growth work, and help others professionally around issues of shame, guilt, and grace.(One colleague even dubbed my work, "Shaw Shame Redemption". Another suggested getting wrist bands that have WWDSD on them: "What Would Doctor Shaw Do?"!) I am a licensed marriage and family therapist in the State of Oregon, and a licensed mental health counselor in Washington. I've served as a pastor for many years, and I currently teach at George Fox University, training professional counselors and marriage and family therapists.

I've been married for over 30 years to my beautiful wife, Karen, and we've got a couple of wonderful kids who are grown. We're a pretty normal family. We love the Oregon coast, college and NFL football, good food, and good friends.

As I continued in my research and writing, I developed a seminar series called *Shame No More*. I have had the honor and privilege to travel many places to teach the *Shame No More* seminars. I never could have imagined that a small-town boy from Nebraska would get the chance to travel to China, Russia, Panama, and Canada, and all around the United States to share about this work. What follows in this book is a written form of what I have taught at universities and churches and wherever anyone would invite me. The stories and lessons presented here have been meaningful to me and to many that have heard them, and I hope they will be meaningful to you.

The past 10 years have seen a rise in awareness about shame in the academic and therapeutic communities. Thanks to the work of Brené Brown and other pioneers in the field of shame study, I am certainly not the first to bring the importance of healing shame to light. I hope, however, that my voice can add to the growing awareness, and that the specific and vital perspective about the church's involvement in this conversation can spark change at every level.

Most of all, I hope that this book will be a companion for

you, in your own journey towards healing and wholeness.

My "Man In The Arena" Moment

If you are a fan of Brené Brown's work, you know that she credits some of her deepest epiphanies to a reading of Theodore Roosevelt's quote, "The Man in the Arena".[1] It's a beautiful quote, to be sure, and a transformative one. I think many of us can look back and recognize similar moments in our lives, where we read or heard or experienced something that altered the course of our destiny.

My moment happened in the midst of reading *The Meaning of Persons* by Paul Tournier in the 1980's. It changed my life forever. Here's what he wrote:

> *When we come honestly and often to keep the tryst with*
> *God, we discover the God of the bible, the personal*
> *God who **cares personally for us**, who **concerns***
> ***himself with us in particular**, who has numbered the*
> *very hairs of our head (Matt 10:30). He does not only*

---

[1] Brown, Brené. *DARING GREATLY: How the Courage to Be Vulnerable Transforms the Way We Live, Love, Parent and Lead*. London, England, Harper and Row Publishing, 2013, pp. 1-3.

*love all men in general, but each of us in particular. He concerns himself not only with our destiny as a whole, but with our every care. He speaks to all men, but has a word for each, calling us as the prophet says, **by our name** (Isaiah 43:1). That is what is meant by a personal relationship.*[2]

I'll never forget the day I read these words. It wasn't that the words were so incredibly more profound than words I had heard or read before. I think it was more that I was ready to understand what they really meant. I was ready to believe that the God of the universe wanted a personal relationship with me, and that it mattered more than anything else in the world.

I was raised in the church and in a Christian family, so I had heard about the love of God my whole life. But I think there is a point in every life where faith becomes personal ... real ... authentic ... for each person. And this was my moment. I believed it. I felt it. My faith wasn't just my family's faith anymore, it was mine. I felt seen, favored, even cherished by the God of the universe.

---

[2] Tournier, Paul. *The Meaning of Persons.* San Francisco, Harper and Row Publishing, 1957, p. 169.

This moment was the beginning of my own freedom from shame.

My prayer is that you will experience a moment like this. Maybe it will come as a result of the words in this book. Maybe it will come as you find your soul settling to watch a beautiful sunset. Maybe it will come as you lift your voice to sing a worship song to God. Maybe it will come as you read and reflect on a scripture and hear it differently than you ever have before. Maybe you've already had this moment with God, and reading my experience serves to remind you of your own.

Whenever your moment is, and however it happens, I pray that you will hold onto it. Don't let it pass you by. May you grasp the reality that *the God of the universe has nothing more important to do than cultivate a personal relationship with you.* God Moments like that are moments when hope comes most fully alive. And that is my prayer, more than anything else: that you will find hope.

In these pages, hope and healing await you!

My prayer is that by engaging your own shame narratives, you will find healing. I pray you will find direction. I pray you will find answers. I pray you will find a belief that things can change, and that your personal relationship with Jesus can deepen and grow. I pray you will have language to talk about your struggles and to work towards your healing. I pray you will know that you are not alone. I pray that you will begin to believe in your own, inherent worth. I pray that you will know that your Heavenly Father loves you so, so much more than you can even imagine!

CHAPTER ONE

Embarrassment, Guilt, and Shame

When I begin to teach my students about shame and grace, I often start with this thought:

Shame is a construct of brokenness.

Grace is a construct of healing.

Meaning, in our work around shame and grace, *shame* is what we are going to use to talk about our brokenness, and *grace* is what we are going to use to talk about our healing. With those words in mind, let's begin to look at the first of these constructs: shame.

Sometimes it's important to define not only what a thing is, but what it is *not*. Shame is similar to embarrassment or guilt, but it is not the same. We are going to begin our work by taking a closer look at all three of these emotions so that we can most accurately understand what shame is. We are all familiar with embarrassment, guilt, and shame, whether we like to reflect upon them or not. These are vital topics to understand and differentiate as we begin to look at the ways they play into our relationships. When we are able to see both how these terms are related to each other and how they're different, we're going to have a basis for understanding everything we are going to learn about shame.

Spiritual Foundation: God's Education and Correction

I love the way Eugene Peterson interprets this passage from Hebrews. This is such an important place to begin as we look at embarrassment, guilt, and shame.

> *My dear child, don't shrug off God's discipline, but don't be crushed by it either. It's the child he loves that he disciplines; the child he embraces, he also corrects.*
>
> *God is educating you; that's why you must never drop out. He's treating you as dear children. This trouble you're in isn't punishment; it's training, the normal experience of children. Only irresponsible parents leave children to fend for themselves. Would you prefer an irresponsible God? We respect our own parents for training and not spoiling us, so why not embrace God's training so we can truly live? While we were children,*

our parents did what seemed best to them. But God is doing what is best for us, training us to live God's holy best. At the time, discipline isn't much fun. It always feels like it's going against the grain. Later, of course, it pays off handsomely, for it's the well-trained who find themselves mature in their relationship with God.

Hebrews 12:5-11 MSG

It's an intriguing and important metaphor to see God as a disciplinarian, but a lot of people have trouble with that. A lot of people have trouble comparing God to their parents, especially in terms of discipline. It's either because their parents genuinely inflicted trauma on them and they sustained long-term wounds because of it, or – more often – it's because most people have a real challenge being honest and authentic with hurts from their past while also remaining loyal to their family. It's really hard for many people to acknowledge guilt or shame from their childhood without casting blame on their parents.

I've been a counselor for over 25 years, and I can tell you that almost every person that I've ever helped, even the ones who were in really difficult places as a result of how they grew up, had parents who did what they thought was best, even when they made some really bad choices in their parenting. Parents do what they think is right; they discipline and communicate in the best ways they know, because they are wired to do the best they can for their kids. Sometimes it does damage, and sometimes it does good.

But God is not doing just what He *thinks* is best for your life. He is truly and completely doing what *is* best. And as this passage suggests, we're in training to become something more than we could ever be on our own. God allows challenges to happen to us in order to bring us to maturity in relationship with Him, and in relationship with every important person in our lives.

Discipline, at least human discipline, can trigger embarrassment, guilt, or shame. After all, it usually means we've done something wrong, and we are experiencing the consequences of our actions. But what I hope to remind us, is that God never desires for us to land in embarrassment, guilt, or shame as a result of discipline. He desires for us to land safely and squarely in His grace, the place where we can learn and grow and thrive in our relationships with others and with Him.

The next verse in the Hebrews passage rounds out this message so beautifully. I like the way the NLT puts it:

> *So take a new grip with your tired hands and stand firm on your shaky legs.*

Hebrews 12:12 NLT

There is hope! There is hope for the exhaustion we feel. There is hope for the shame we carry. There is hope that our Father God, who loves us personally and individually, will see us through our story and into freedom and wholeness. As we look into these three core human experiences of embarrassment, guilt, and shame, let's remember that we are journeying beyond them into the wide, open spaces of grace.

Embarrassment

Mark Twain once said, "Man is the only animal that blushes - or needs to."[3] I think he was probably right about that. We humans do a pretty good job of embarrassing ourselves all too frequently. You can probably remember the last time you had a piece of food stuck in your teeth, or a trail of toilet paper following you out of the bathroom, or a slip of the tongue in an important conversation. That feeling that comes over us in the moment we realize we have broken a social contract or norm is something that we all are familiar with.

In my experience, there are four conditions that come

---

[3] Downey, Charles. "Taking the Chagrin Out of Embarrassment." *Oregonian.* 2000.

together in order to create a scenario that produces embarrassment.

1.   A **failure**

2.   That happens **suddenly**

3.   In front of a **public**

4.   Whose opinion you **value**[4]

So, for embarrassment to happen, we have to fail, to blow it, to do something that violates an expectation or norm. It has to happen suddenly, meaning it has to happen quickly enough so that we don't have a chance to recover or to do something to change it in some way. It needs to be public, in front of other people, and we have to value - at some level - that public's opinion. When those four things are in place, embarrassment always follows.

One of my favorite stories of embarrassment is about a British diplomat who was preparing to stand and give a speech in front of his peers. As he began to rise to take the stage, he realized that the fly was open on his trousers. He saw it in time to close it, so he sat back down quickly to pull the zipper shut. But as he did, he caught the edge of his tie in the zipper. When he stood, the tie pulled tightly around his neck and he began to choke! The audience didn't know what

---

[4] Downey, Charles. "Taking the Chagrin Out of Embarrassment." *Oregonian.*2000.

was going on, and thought he was having a heart attack. Finally, the host of the event realized what had happened and cut the tie before it completely choked him. The poor fellow had to leave the room with half of his tie hanging from his neck and the other half hanging from his fly. As you can imagine, word of this event traveled quickly within the diplomatic community, and he became known for and teased about this episode for quite some time.[5]

I can't ever tell this story in a teaching setting without cracking up, because it is pretty hilarious to picture. But there is a part of me that feels some empathetic embarrassment for the guy! I'm pretty good at playing off my own embarrassing moments, but I can imagine how I would feel if that happened to me. I wear far fewer ties now than I used to, for more reasons than one!

My Own Story

I suppose it's not fair to share the stories of other people's embarrassing moments without also sharing my own. I'll give a fair word of warning before I do – it's mildly inappropriate. I'm sorry about that, but then again, I suppose that most

---

[5] Downey, Charles. "Taking the Chagrin Out of Embarrassment." *Oregonian.* 2000.

embarrassing stories are mildly inappropriate, since they involve breaking social norms of … well … appropriateness.

So, here's my story. It was my first year of teaching at George Fox University, over 25 years ago. I was a brand-new professor, totally over my head with genuinely no idea what I was doing. I was sort of in that "fake it 'til you make it" phase of work induction, about to go before a bunch of graduate students and impart to them all of the knowledge they were hoping to acquire. It felt important to me that the students get a chance to meet their new professor before we delved into the academia, so I attended a pizza party that the university hosted for all students and faculty, to give us a chance to socialize and connect before the first class.

The students were as nervous as I was, since it was their first day back to school for the semester, and for some it was their first day of grad school altogether. None of us knew quite what to expect, so it was awkward all around, but we sat there in a big room filled with tables, making conversation and eating pizza.

I ended up seated at a table with six or eight middle-aged women. I was young, they were nervous, and it was a very awkward conversation. Finally, we settled on a topic that interested all of us: the Myers-Briggs Type Indicator test. It's one of those tests out there that gives people a way to talk about personality traits and types.[6] With Myers-Briggs, people are categorized by different letter combinations: *J* stands for judging, *P* stands for perceiving, *E* means extrovert, *I* means introvert, and so on.

As we were in the midst of the conversation, one of the women at the table said, "I'm a little nervous about going back to graduate school because I've been out of school for a long time and I'm not very organized. I'm going to have to work on my *J-ness*."

By that, she meant that she wanted to work on that part of her personality, her *J-ness*, her judgment of herself and the way it affected her organization and detail awareness.

Now, the opposite of J is P. Without even hesitating, my extroverted self said, "Oh, that's not a problem for me. I'm going to have to work on my *P-ness*."

Absolute silence struck the table.

Go ahead...say that line again, out loud. Yes. This is what I said.

I sat for a moment and let the word *P-ness* reverberate in my mind. It felt like an hour, but in reality, it was about six

---

[6] Briggs Myers, Isabel. *Introduction to Type: A guide to understanding your results on the MBTI Instrument*. Cpp, Inc., 6th edition, 1996.

seconds. I imagined what those poor women must have been trying to conjure as a response to their professor saying something so absurd, and my face turned beet red.

Finally, they burst into laughter, and I laughed right along with them. We chuckled away the awkward tension of the whole episode and I left them with, "Wow, that pretty much said it all, didn't it?"

They agreed, and the embarrassment was over. We went to class and we all lived happily ever after. Nobody fired me or anything!

I would not keep telling this story if my colleagues did not keep telling it on me. They keep it alive, so I figure if they're going to have that much fun telling it on me, certainly I get to tell it on myself and have a little bit of fun with it as well.

We all relate to being embarrassed, and I'm sure as you read that story, you might have felt some empathic embarrassment as well. When we feel embarrassed, most of us turn red, or blush. It's actually a healthy human response to an embarrassing situation – our blush indicates that we are aware of our mistake and feel uncomfortable with it. It actually gives comfort to those who witness an embarrassing episode when they see the perpetrator acknowledge the embarrassment with a blush.

Some intriguing research was done about this at the

University of Washington.[7] A group of psychologists went to several large grocery retailers, like Costco and Walmart, and they set up a pyramid of toilet paper at the end of an aisle in the store. Imagine that! A pyramid of toilet paper! This experiment took place a number of years ago ... I suppose in 2020 they wouldn't have picked such a hot commodity to use so frivolously!

Anyhow, they rigged it so that when people went by, anybody who grabbed a package of toilet paper would cause the whole pyramid of toilet paper to come crashing down. As you can imagine, this caused a lot of immediate embarrassment!

Not only did they observe the people as the incidents happened, they went back and interviewed both the people who knocked over the pyramid of toilet paper and bystanders who watched it happen. As you might imagine, the people who knocked over the pyramids of toilet paper were upset, frustrated, and irritated. They were embarrassed, they blushed, they turned red, they couldn't believe they had done such a humiliating thing. That's kind of what we would expect.

But what is most interesting is that when they interviewed the folks who had *watched* the people knock over the pyramids of

---

[7] Downey, Charles. "Taking the Chagrin Out of Embarrassment." *Oregonian.* 2000.

toilet paper, the number one thing they found was *empathy*. They found care, compassion, understanding. The people who witnessed the embarrassing moment felt favorably toward the person who caused it. Isn't that intriguing?

If you are the one that is embarrassed, the one who is turning red, you might assume that if you feel a certain way about yourself, everyone else probably feels the same way about you, too. But this research suggests the opposite. It suggests that when I feel bad about myself, there can actually be people around me who feel really good about me.

That's an encouragement for us to realize that even when we are going through something difficult, there may be other people who are caring for us and connect with us.

Embarrassment is natural and good. It happens to us in real-time, but it doesn't stick with us long enough to do lasting damage to our souls. If it does, then it is no longer embarrassment. It's turned into something else: guilt or shame.

Guilt

Guilt and shame often get used interchangeably. Sometimes we say guilt, but we really mean shame, or vice-versa. In reality, these two terms are vastly different. The difference between guilt and shame is simple: **what I do** versus **who I am**. Guilt is about our behavior, while shame is about our identity. Lewis Smedes puts it this way, "The difference between guilt and shame is very close-in theory. We feel guilty for what we do. We feel shame for what we are... we may feel guilty because we lied to our mother. We may feel shame because we are not the person our mother wanted us to be."[8]

Guilt is a "mature feeling of regret [when one]has violated a personal value",[9] or when we have done something that we don't believe we should have done. Guilt is the natural and healthy response we feel when we do something that goes against our moral standards or against our values and beliefs. Guilt focuses on our behaviors and our values, and how those two things line up. If a person is capable of experiencing guilt, they have developed some inner rules and a conscience.

If you are having an experience of guilt, you can feel badly about your behavior but still have respect for yourself. Guilt does not take a situation and extrapolate an identity. Guilt simply looks at the situation and allows a feeling of regret.

---

[8] Smedes, Lewis. **Shame and Grace**. New York, Zondervan Publishing, 1993, pp. 9-10.

[9] Fossum, Merle & Mason, Marilyn. **Facing Shame: Families in Recovery**. New York, WW Norton and Company, 1986, p. 5.

When I was 16 years old, I had a 1970, red and white Pontiac LeMans. And it was fast. It had a 3-speed hurst shift, a big motor, chrome wheels … this was the 80's, by the way. And this car was *sweet*. It would just tear the tires when you stepped on the accelerator. It was probably too much car for a 16-year-old boy to have – but gosh, I loved that car.

I raced only once, and I won. I never had to race again, because the stories of how fast that car was reverberated throughout the high school.

One day, as 16-year-old boys often do, I was driving a bit recklessly. I punched it, and it fishtailed, and I couldn't control the car. I ended up in the ditch, tearing up the front fender. As I waited for help to get it out of the ditch, I could only imagine all the trouble I was in. I went straight home and just handed the keys to my dad before even telling him the story of what I had done.

I felt guilty about my behavior, and I knew that it would cost me. I was right. I lost privileges to the car for a month, and I had to work to pay for the damage I had done to my own car. I had to ride the bus to school, I couldn't date or hang out with friends on the weekends. Because I had made a wrong, destructive choice, there were consequences that I had to face.

But my behavior didn't get shamed. I wasn't told there was something wrong with me because of what I had done. I had to make amends. I had to face the reality of my choices. I felt guilt, and the guilt I felt was a healthy response to what had happened.

So, we've looked at embarrassment, which is healthy and normal. It's frequently silly and short-lived; it doesn't exact a lasting toll on our psyches. We've looked at guilt, which is also healthy and normal. It's part of our inner conscience, and part of our decision-making. When we take an action that produces guilt, we can usually remedy the feelings with an apology and by taking whatever restorative steps are necessary. While long-term, repeated feelings of guilt might do some lasting damage in our hearts and minds, it's usually not the guilt doing the damage, but its far more sinister counterpart: shame.

Shame

Shame is about identity. It is the belief that something is wrong with *who we are*. People feel shame around all kinds of experiences. Shame attaches itself to trauma. Abuse, rape, shootings, all kinds of deeply inappropriate behaviors that are done to us. And shame hangs around all kinds of other deeply hard experiences that we often don't think of as trauma. It could be triggered by getting fired, or by an addiction. It could stem from parenting failures, or a marriage that ends in divorce. Sometimes it happens after a DUI or an affair. Dropping out of school or failing to get good grades can bring about experiences of shame. People feel shame about not being pretty enough, thin enough, smart enough, or successful enough. We find all kinds of places where we decide that we're not good enough - in our own eyes or in somebody else's eyes – and we experience shame because of it.

Shame is not like embarrassment or guilt. It is not healthy. It is not helpful. It does not pass in and out of our minds based on singular experiences. Shame sticks. It accuses, it condemns, and it destroys.

Shame is the most damaging and devastating human experience ever.

I remember in my early years of counseling, a man I'll call George came in to see me. On the outside, this man was wildly successful. He had a beautiful wife and kids, he was killing it at work, his social life and church life appeared to be flourishing. At first, I was having a hard time identifying what was really troubling him.

About five or six sessions into our counseling, he looked at me and he said, "I'm going to tell you something that nobody knows. Every night when I go in to put my two daughters to bed, I tuck them in, and they go to sleep, and life is great." He waits a minute, and then he says, "About a half hour after they go to sleep, I go back in, and I give them a little kiss on the forehead, and I whisper something in their ear. I say, 'Honey, I hope when you grow up, you don't marry someone like your dad.'"

It broke my heart. The tears overtook him as he began telling me all the ways that he was failing and the places where he wasn't measuring up to his own standards. He had such a heavy load of shame that he literally told his daughters every night not to marry a man like him.

After some time talking and processing, I challenged him. I said, "George, this week, I want you to try whispering something different when you go back in there and give your girls a kiss on the forehead. I want you to say, "Honey, I pray that when you grow up, you meet and marry a man like the dad that I'm becoming."

I said, "George, you're working on it, you're trying to make changes in your life and deal with those places inside that make you feel the way that you do. And I want you to be encouraged and hopeful about the changes that can happen. I want you to believe that your daughters could meet and fall in love with someone like *you* and the person that you're becoming."

The next week when he came in, he told me that he was able to do it a couple of times that week, but that it was really hard for him to start thinking of himself in that way. I challenged him to start saying this every night. Slowly, as we worked on the areas in his life that were causing his shame, it began to get easier for him to believe that he was a worthy husband and father. We worked on it for a long time.

As I was closing out a counseling session with George, months later, I asked him if he remembered that first breakthrough moment. He did. And I said, "What do you tell your daughters now when you go in at the end of the night?"

He got a big smile on his face and he said, "I tell them I love them, and I can't wait for them to grow up and marry someone like the dad that I'm becoming."

Done. I'm done at that point! I mean, *how much better does it get?* This guy was in the process of being freed of his shame! And by the way, they don't all go that way. Just for the record, not everyone experiences such a clear victory over their shame. This guy worked hard to deal with some deep pain, and it was rewarding to see God redeeming it and releasing him from his shame.

There's another chapter to this story, and it just keeps getting better. Not long ago, after a number of years, George came back for a second round of counseling. His daughters are now teenagers, and recently we've started talking about what he will whisper in their ears when he walks them down the aisle. I can relate deeply to this, as I recently walked my own daughter down the aisle. What a priceless, precious, holy moment.

We helped him think through what he wanted to tell them in that moment, and George plans to say something like this: "Honey, I love you so much, and I am so proud of you and the man you are preparing to marry! And do you know what? He's a little bit like me!"

That just makes me smile. What a journey of healing.

But how many of us think similar thoughts about ourselves? How many of us want our child to marry a person like us? How many of us are living under the weight of the accusation and condemnation of shame?

When I give lectures about shame, I invite people to share their shame experiences. Here are a few I've heard over the years:

> *I remember feeling shame about being poor. When I was in grade school, I got reduced cost lunches and I had to go to a special place in the cafeteria to get those. I stood out in ways that I didn't want to, and I felt*

shame about that.

I remember a parent telling me, "Your sister isn't as smart as you are, and she gets straight A's. What's wrong with you?" I hated that.

I remember when I was three or four years old, I had a swimming teacher who shamed me because I was afraid to swim. She didn't know that I had almost drowned the year before. She made me sit on the side of the pool, and she treated me like a baby.

When I was a young boy, I got spanked so hard and long that it broke the skin on my legs and my backside. This was done while I was in a compromised position, with my pants down and with people watching. I was so ashamed!

When I was in fifth grade, I struggled with math. The teacher arranged the class so that all the slow kids were on one side of the room. I was one of those kids. Everyone knew who sat where in that class, and what it meant. I hated going to math.

The Distinction Between Shame and Guilt

Let's look once more at shame versus guilt, so that we can really narrow in on shame for the rest of our study. Tangney & Dearing say there are four primary categories that differentiate shame and guilt: focus, experience, concern, and motivational response.[10]

The **focus** of guilt is on the behavior: "*I did* this horrible thing." The focus of shame is on the person: "*I am* horrible." In order to determine if someone is feeling shame or guilt, we have to look at whether they are fixated on the situation at hand, or on themselves.

The **experiences** of guilt and shame are different. Guilt experiences *inner tension* that feels like remorse or regret. It says, "I made a mistake, I want to make amends, I want to avoid that behavior in the future. Shame experiences *inner condemnation* that feels like punishment. Shame says, "I want to disappear, I want to get small. I feel worthless. I feel powerless. I can never fix this."

In regard to the way we relate with other people, there is also a major difference between shame and guilt. Our **concern** with shame is ourselves; our concern with guilt is others.

---

[10] Tangney, June & Dearing, Rhonda. *Shame and Guilt*. New York, Guilford Press, 2003. Kindle edition.

Shame is all about *me*. It's narcissistic and ego-driven, concerned with how others see me and how I see myself. Guilt is actually about *others*, noticing the effects of my words and behavior on someone else.

We also have different **responses** to guilt versus shame. When we feel guilt, our response is usually to face it. We apologize, we make amends, we seek restoration and then we move on. When we are dealing with shame, we run. We want to hide, to escape, to punish ourselves or the ones who have shamed us.

A Prayer

As we wrap up this first chapter, I'm hoping you are thinking about embarrassment, and how those temporarily mortifying moments can bring levity and even connection with and compassion from others. I hope you're making sense of guilt being a helpful feeling, something related to our consciences, something that can correct us and help us do things different and better as we move forward in relationships and in life.

And I hope that the concept of shame is also making some sense personally for you. What is it for you? How does it manifest in your life? What triggers it? What places inside you are operating under a narrative of condemnation that you are not enough? Those places are the places we want to spend some time with, and hopefully invite God into to make a difference in your life and in your relationships.

When I teach this material to students and professionals, I often end each session with a prayer. If this is meaningful to you, let me pray grace over you today.

> *Dear Jesus, we know that you are a God of love. We know that you do not desire to see your children trapped by the lies of shame; you desire to see us freed by the truth of grace. You want to come alongside every one of us and bring healing and change into places of our own personal shame. Use this book, use our relationships, use people and circumstances today and moving forward beyond today. Bring truth into our lives in a way that will make a difference. Restore our relationship with you. Restore every relationship we have in our lives that has been ravaged by shame. Show us the unconditional love that you have for us, so that we may adopt it for ourselves as well. We give you the praise and the glory for every step we take towards freedom. Amen.*

CHAPTER TWO

A Closer Look at Shame

The reality is that *everyone* experiences shame. *Everyone* experiences brokenness. We don't all experience it in the same way or to the same degree. Our backgrounds and the challenges we have faced in life define some of our shame. Our personalities and the way we understand and process things define some of our shame. Our wounds and trauma define some of our shame. Our relationships and the health or dysfunction we experience there define some of our shame.

Shame is a way of talking about our brokenness. And we are all broken. My invitation to you is this:

Lean into your brokenness.

Be brave with me, and look shame right in the face. As we do, we will see not only our brokenness, but the path to our healing. This is the way of grace.

Spiritual Foundation: Readiness

Before we can truly do the work of addressing our shame and moving towards an experience of grace, we have to be ready. Let's see what Jesus had to say about it:

> The disciples came up and asked, "Why do you tell stories?"
>
> He replied, "You've been given insight into God's kingdom. You know how it works. Not everybody has this gift, this insight; it hasn't been given to them. Whenever someone has a ready heart for this, the insights and understandings flow freely. But if there is no readiness, any trace of receptivity soon disappears. That's why I tell stories: to create readiness, to nudge the people toward receptive insight. In their present state they can stare till doomsday and not see it, listen till they're blue in the face and not get it. I don't want Isaiah's forecast repeated all over again:
>
> Your ears are open but you don't hear a thing.
> Your eyes are awake but you don't see a thing.
> The people are blockheads!
> They stick their fingers in their ears
> so they won't have to listen;
> They screw their eyes shut so they won't have to look,

so they won't have to deal with me face-to-face and let me heal them.

"But you have God-blessed eyes—eyes that see! And God-blessed ears—ears that hear! A lot of people, prophets and humble believers among them, would have given anything to see what you are seeing, to hear what you are hearing, but never had the chance.

Matthew 13:10-17 MSG

You may be reading this book from a place of total readiness. You may be totally prepared to take action on the things you are going to engage as a part of this process. I see people like that come to my seminars all the time. They are keyed up and ready, taking copious notes and asking questions at every opportunity. They are alert and leaning in, ready to receive, learn, and implement. That is a state of extreme readiness.

You may also be reading this book from a different place. You may not be entirely ready to fully explore your experiences of shame. It may feel painful or triggering for you, or you might just feel confused or overwhelmed about where and how to begin. I see people like that in my seminars all the time, too. They are the ones who come with their notebooks closed, their arms crossed, their eyes averted. They may be absorbing some of the content, but it's clear that an internal block is stopping a lot of it from getting through.

I'm here to tell you something important today: wherever you are on the spectrum of readiness today is okay. It's okay. To quote a life coach friend of mine: "Be where you are. Move when you're ready."[11]

It is okay to be where you are. And it is good to move when you're ready.

But look at what Jesus says in this passage: he tells stories to help people *increase their readiness*. That's what this book is. It's a collection of stories and experiences, combined with research and teaching, to help increase our readiness as we move along the path from shame to grace.

I bet something like the following story has happened to you. You've had a conversation with somebody significant in your life and you've told them something they need to do, something they need to change, something they need to think differently about. And you've said it over and over and over to them, and they have looked at you with a blank stare and never taken any action on that thing.

Then that person that you've talked to goes to, oh, I don't

---

[11] NeSmith, Erin. https://www.growintoyoufoundation.org. Accessed 27 June 2021.

know, a Shame No More seminar, or to church, or talks to somebody else. And they hear something profoundly similar to what you have already told them, only they come home talking about it like it's the first time they've heard the thing! They talk about how ready they are to take action, and how right that person who said it was, and how brilliant it was. And you think to yourself that they must be kidding! You've been telling them this for years, and they have never listened, but now that someone else is saying it, it's brilliant?

An experience like that isn't about the person who was speaking the truth being brilliant. It's about the person receiving the truth being ready to hear it!

So, wherever you are today, it's okay. Be where you are. Move when you're ready. And allow the stories, illustrations, teachings, and insight in this book to move you along the path of readiness.

There's one other dynamic to this passage that's important to mention, and that's the act of denial. Of course, as a counselor, I see denial all the time. Look at the way the scripture puts it: "They stick their fingers in their ears so they won't have to listen; they screw their eyes shut, so they won't have to look." That's denial.

Every one of us practices at least a little bit of denial with things that are really difficult for us to deal with emotionally or relationally. We pretend we don't see them; we sweep them under the rug, and we convince ourselves and those around us that we are fine. Or maybe we over-spiritualize our problems, and think we just need to pray more and wait on God. There's nothing wrong with prayer, of course; we should all pray lots more than we probably do. But prayer as denial, pretending like we just don't have to do anything and that God will just magically take care of everything, can be detrimental to our hearts and our relationships.

If we look at the very last piece of this scripture, we see something pretty beautiful. God isn't asking us to look our problems in the face so that we can feel shame over them, is He? "They screw their eyes shut so they won't have to look, so they won't have to deal with me face-to-face and *let me heal them*." Do you see? This is the path from shame to grace. This is the path from brokenness to healing. Dealing with God face-to-face, engaging our shame with authenticity and vulnerability, is what will free us to walk in grace.

Why, when we are faced with the opportunity of receiving healing, would we walk away from it? Because it's scary, because it's uncomfortable, and because we don't know what's going to come next. We long for healing and we're afraid of it at the very same time. Whatever our family of origin situation was, we got comfortable with it. We got used to it. And guess what we do today? We recreate it in our current relationships because we know what to do in that environment. Even if it was amazingly unhealthy, maybe we got great at putting out those particular types of fires. Maybe we got used to handling crisis because that's what it was all the time. Maybe we learned to function in the dysfunction, and now we keep creating the very dysfunction that traps us in our shame.

God is offering us healing and breakthrough. And it is a normal, human response to be afraid of that healing and breakthrough. We see it in the scripture, we see it in our family, and we see it in ourselves. Shame keeps us locked into patterns of brokenness that have never served us well, and God desires to heal us and to set us free.

My invitation to you is to normalize the fear that you may feel about looking into your own shame. Normalize the reality that you simply *are where you are* on the path of readiness. And then, listen to the invitation of God. Listen to the stories, listen to the insight, listen between the lines of this book. Allow your heart to open to the reality that as you choose to deal with God face-to-face and engage your shame, the result will be your healing.

Be where you are. Move when you're ready.

Talking about Shame

When I began my work in shame research over 30 years ago, it was not a topic that many clinicians or professionals had much training in. In fact, even today, most counselors and therapists have never taken a course on shame. You will probably know more after reading this book than most professionals do. Research suggests that it's hard to get specialized help regarding shame, because there are so few professionals who have specific training and education in it. Furthermore, the work of the church regarding shame is equally lacking. Pastors and counselors in the Christian community are also untrained in helping people to work through their shame, and the reality is that a good portion of the church has actually done more damage by *causing* shame rather than healing it.

Thanks to the work of Brené Brown and other writers and researchers, the topic is gaining some traction in both the academic and therapeutic communities, but we still have a long way to go, especially in the church. There is something inherently difficult in talking about and working with shame. I believe it's because in order to really help someone else through their own experience of shame, the clinician or professional has to do their own work first. They have to deal with their own shame before they can ethically and effectively do shame work with other people.

Because of this, shame is a silent epidemic.

And we are afraid to talk about it. Many of us don't have a lot of safe people or places in our lives that we can go to talk through our shame. We don't want to share deeply about these things with just anybody, because these things are at the core of our identities and worth. So we keep it hidden, like those people in the scriptures, and we screw our eyes shut and stick our fingers in our ears so that we won't have to deal with it.

The reality is that the less we talk about our shame and brokenness, the more control it has in our lives. The things that stay dark and hidden begin to drive us; they become a part of our motivation, a part of our intentions, a part of our perceptions. And sometimes – actually most of the time – we don't even realize how powerful that brokenness is, and how it is influencing our relationships.

The spoken word is always powerful and always healing when it comes to shame. Every time we say hard things out loud, we take a step toward healing.

It's time to talk about our shame.

Experiences of Shame

Remember, shame attaches itself to trauma. Emotional, physical, or sexual abuse, and many dramatic relational and life experiences end up leaving serious cuts, scars, and emotional residue of shame long after the event is over. We often think of shame as something caused by a traumatic and abusive experience, and there is certainly shame that comes from those places. But shame can also come from lots of normal experiences where we just feel like we're not good enough.

Here is a list of some things that can trigger shame:[12]

- Getting fired
- Being in recovery
- Filing bankruptcy
- Having out of control kids
- Being single
- Getting divorced
- Having an affair
- Getting a DUI
- Struggling with infertility

---

[12] This list is inspired by and partially curated from: Brown, Brené. *DARING GREATLY: How the Courage to Be Vulnerable Transforms the Way We Live, Love, Parent and Lead*. London, England, Harper and Row Publishing, 2013, pp. 69-70.

- Acting out with pornography
- Flunking out of school
- Not being attractive enough
- Not being smart or successful enough

You may relate to both traumatic experiences and "normal" day to day experiences of shame. They are both deep, difficult, personal cuts. We could probably keep adding to that list for a long time. As you read it, there might be something there that jumps out at you, or you might get some clarity about what your particular story would add to this list. That's a good thing. Seeing experiences in your life that have caused shame is a part of healing it.

Here are some synonyms for shame:

Synonyms for Shame

- Humiliated
- Embarrassed
- Dishonored
- Shy
- Self-conscious
- Inferior
- Low Self Esteem
- Guilty
- Degraded
- Inadequate
- Not Good Enough

Brené Brown writes, "Shame is the intensely painful feeling or experience of believing we are flawed and therefore unworthy of love and belonging."[13]

Shame can show up in a lot of different ways. Let's look at a few of the most common.

Shame can be a sense of **insufficiency**. It can be the inner voice that says, "I'm not good enough. I'm not worthy enough. I'm not competent enough. And I can never be any of those things, *enough*." This insufficiency leaves us feeling hopeless, because we believe there is no way to move ourselves from who we are to who we think we need to be.

Shame can also arise from teachings about our **unworthiness** in our relationship with God. If we hear often that we're never good enough, we can never earn His love, even though He longs to give that to us, then we can end up trying to earn his love. And when we are trying to earn the love of God, we are certainly also trying to earn the love of others. This experience of shame leaves us always striving but never succeeding in our relationships, believing that we will never be worth loving.

---

[13] Brown, Brené. https://brenebrown.com/blog/2013/01/14/shame-v-guilt/.Accessed 27 June 2021.

Shame can also be caused by **forced emotional exposure**: being revealed or "outed" when we least want that to happen. We feel judged and exposed, on display for all the world to see. This can damage us severely. I can't help but think of two places where that can happen on a regular basis, places that are supposed to be the safest places ever - a counselor's office and the church. And yet, sadly, I can't tell you how many people have been shamed in counselors' offices and in churches.

One major reason why shame is so powerful and damaging is in its ability to make us feel alone, cut off, removed from others and from God. Whether we experience shame as insufficiency or unworthiness or exposure, it leads us to believe that we are better off alone. It causes us to isolate, or to act out in ways that drive our loved ones away from us. One of the saddest parts of shame is that it is a self-fulfilling prophesy. When we believe something is true, eventually, it does indeed become true.

Who is the Judge?

We've already looked a little bit at the differences between guilt and shame, but we need to look at another one that is really important. As we give language to this and tell some stories about it, it's going to help us see the places where shame has a grip of power in our lives.

One of the ways to illuminate an experience of shame is ask ourselves the question: "Who is the judge"?

Guilt has an internal judge. When we develop in a healthy way, we develop a sense of values. We learn to believe that we can change what we are doing when it violates our own moral code. If something I do goes against what I believe I'm supposed to do, that's guilt. That's an internal judge. When we experience our internal judge, it can still be painful. We don't like the feeling that we have violated our own moral code. And sometimes we might get stuck in our own guilt for a while and punish ourselves for whatever it was that turned us away from true north on our moral compass. Underneath that feeling of guilt, however, is the belief that we can make a change. We believe that we are capable of following our own code of values, and we eventually take steps to continue to follow it.

Shame has an external judge. Experiences of shame go beyond an internal moral compass or sense of values. We give *other people* the power to judge us, and power is a huge player in shame. When we feel shame, we believe that there is an external moral code, something *beyond what we are capable* of achieving. We can deal with this external judge one of two ways.

One way is to be constantly worried and afraid of what others think of us. And even deeper than that, we fear that we are not fooling the ones to whom we have given the power. We might send ourselves on a lifelong quest to trick the powers that be (our pastor, our family, our spouse, our boss, our therapist) into believing that we are living up to the code, but all the while, underneath, we know we never will. We obsess about what they think about us and if they believe we are measuring up, and yet we feel like it's all a dog and pony show that we have to keep up so they don't see our true colors.

However, the total opposite can also be true. We might decide that we couldn't care less about what anyone thinks of us. We might decide that we aren't going to put on a show at all, and we are never going to allow ourselves to worry about what anyone believes about us. This might sound healthier, but if it's driven by shame, the same damage is done. Underneath, our reasons for this come down to the devastating reality that we believe we are simply not capable of measuring up. We believe we aren't worthy of love and belonging, as Brené Brown puts it. And so, we just don't try.

Either way, the power lies outside of ourselves, because the judgment comes from outside of ourselves.

When we are taking responsibility for our own behaviors, our own actions, our own intentions, our own thoughts, our own processes, we can experience freedom from shame. As we take that responsibility, we internalize the assessment of our own selves and our own lives, rather than surrendering that power and living in shame.

Shame Triggers

I'm a football player – or at least, I was a football player in my younger days. When I played defense, I was supposed to react to the ball. Meaning, I was supposed to take immediate action driven by something outside of myself. Reaction might work well on the football field, but it doesn't always work very well in life and relationships. When I react in life and relationships, it's quick. It's impatient. It's not thoughtful. It's impelled by something outside of me and it causes me to act in a way that I may regret later.

When I respond, it's a little slower, a little more patient, a little more on purpose. In the context of human relationships, response is a far better and healthier plan than reaction.

Shame causes us to *react* emotionally, while guilt prompts us to *respond* emotionally.

Not only that, but guilt responds *proportionately* to an action, event, or circumstance. Shame reacts *disproportionate*ly to an action, event, or circumstance. A trivial event can trigger massive feelings of shame.

I bet you've had an interaction with someone where, whatever the event was, it wasn't a very big deal. Maybe you and your spouse are running late to church, due to reasons that may or may not be inside your control. And while it's not ideal to be running late to church, it's not a huge problem, either. On a problem magnitude scale of one to ten, running late to church is probably a "one" or a "two". But what if your spouse acts like it's an "eight" or a "nine"? What if the verbalization surrounding the event sounds like it's the actual end of the world?

You might feel like it makes no sense, because, in your estimation, this problem is only a "one" or a "two". There's something more going on when the size of an event is that small and the size of the reaction is that big.

Or maybe you are the one who has a massive reaction to a small problem. You forget to make a phone call to your child's school to give them some information. Okay, this might get up to a "three" or a "four", since it's about your kids. But you find yourself spiraling into a panic because to you it feels like a "nine" or a "ten", and you don't even know why! You don't even understand why this feels like the biggest failure the world has ever seen.

This is what we call a *shame trigger*. This wasn't just about the current circumstance. It's not just about being late for church or forgetting to make a phone call. These circumstances are prompting a reaction, but that reaction is based on a whole lot of past shame. The circumstance touches or prods or pushes on that shame, and you get triggered. It happens to all of us.

When I experience conflicts or upsetting circumstances in my life, and I sense myself preparing to either react or respond, I ask myself this question:

On a scale of one to ten, how big of problem was this?

If I have a fight with my significant other, I ask myself how big a fight it was. Was it a little one, a medium one, or a big one? What number is it on the problem magnitude scale? And then I ask myself another question:

What was my emotional reaction to the problem?

The goal is for my emotional reaction/response to follow the size of the event. If I have a "five" event and I have a "five" emotional reaction to it, that's relatively healthy. That's kind of normal. But if find myself having "one" and "two" events where I am dumping "eight", "nine", or "ten" emotional reactions, then there's something more going on inside of me. I've got some internal work to do.

Several years ago, right after the holidays, I was taking a lamp back to Target. There I was, in line with half of the world, trying to make a post-Christmas return. In front of me, there was another guy who was also returning a lamp. I guess lamps were a big-ticket item that year. But the man in front of me had purchased the lamp weeks ago, and he didn't have a receipt or any way of tracking his purchase. As he spoke to the customer service rep, he demanded the full $50 back that he spent on the lamp.

The nice woman behind the counter said, "I'm so sorry sir, but since you've bought the lamp, we have marked it down four times. It's now on clearance. We now sell that same lamp for $19.99, so that's what I can refund you today."

Now, this is a problem, right? That's upsetting. Of course, the guy wants his full $50 back. But this is like a "one" or a "two" sort of a problem. Thirty dollars is not worth getting arrested over. But this guy almost did. He had a total meltdown right there in the Target checkout line. I was embarrassed, I was worried for everyone's safety, I was totally shocked because he took this thing to level "ten". There was clearly some underlying shame issues around justice and fairness that this guy needed to work through.

It can go the other way, too. I remember sitting in my office with a client one day, trying to illustrate this idea for her. I'll call her Jane. As I was sharing with Jane about this reacting versus responding idea and about the problem magnitude scale, she began to tell me about a circumstance at work. She was facing a very irritating, frustrating, difficult situation with a co-worker. The problem that she described to me was probably an "eight". It was very challenging, but she told me that her emotional reaction was actually about a "three".

I knew something was going on, even though this was a small reaction to a big problem. After we talked for a while and she thought about why her reaction had been so small, she found some clarity. She said, "Okay, I stuffed it. I stuffed it, because I knew I couldn't deal with that person in that environment. So, I just smiled and stuffed it."

We call that denial.

That makes perfect sense. There are times in life when we have little problems and we dump big reactions on them. There are times in life when we have big problems and we dump little reactions on them. In either of these cases, our brokenness is causing us to react in unhealthy ways.

That sort of brokenness is driven by the shame that we carry.

The Shame Backpack

Let's think about it this way. We all go through life with an imaginary, invisible backpack on. You didn't know it, but you've got a backpack on right now. So do I.

Difficult things are going to happen to you today, and this week. And every time something difficult happens, whether it's a problem, a fight, a miscommunication, or whatever, you put the emotion of that experience in the backpack. Sometimes you deal with the emotion right then, and the only thing you have to put in the backpack is a processed memory. But sometimes you need to stuff it, when you can't deal with it right in the moment, so you just put it in the backpack for later. You save this up in your backpack, and if you save it long enough, it turns into shame.

And then sometimes, another event happens, maybe a small one, you reach back and pull stuff out of the backpack, and you dump it on this new, smaller circumstance. The shame trigger hits you and your backpack is full, so the only response is to let the shame spill out.

All the time, we're putting stuff in and taking stuff out of our backpacks. And sometimes, it's the safest places in our lives where it all comes spilling out. Let's say I have an interchange with my boss that doesn't go well. In the moment, I can't really talk back, because I don't want to get fired. So, I stuff some of that emotional reaction into my shame backpack. I'm kind of hurt, and I'm kind of angry, and I'm kind of embarrassed. So, I stuff it in my backpack, and then I go home.

What do I do when I go home? The same thing we all do. We go to the safest, most caring, most loving people in our lives. Husbands, wives, best friends, family. What do we do? We dump stuff on them that's not theirs. We unleash the contents of our shame backpacks on the people who love us, and in turn, we *create more shame.*

If I go home to my wife and verbally attack her for some offhanded comment she made, I'm letting my shame backpack explode on her. She doesn't deserve that, nor does she understand it. In her mind the comment was a "one", but in my mind it's a "ten", because my backpack can't fit anything else. The reality is that most of my response has absolutely nothing to do with her, but I can't control it because I'm still feeling shame about what happened at work.

My shame is causing me to alienate myself and reinforce the narrative of my own unworthiness. There's that self-fulfilling prophecy thing again!

By the end of this book, my prayer is that we will all be able to see these backpacks for what they are. And while we'll always have the backpack on - because that way of processing is just part of being human – we sure can work on some healthy ways of going through the work of emptying it.

A Lens on Life: The Way We SEE Self, Relationships, The Church, and The World

We have a couple phrases in our house that we call "Dad Statements". My kids are grown now, but when they were growing up, there were two expressions they heard nearly every day. I also have them posted on the walls in my counseling office, because I need to be surrounded by the truth. It doesn't hurt my clients and colleagues either! I say these phrases pretty often, because we all need the reminding. The first is this:

Life is not fair.

I've told my kids, I've told my clients, and I'm telling you now … life is not fair. I wish I could tell you that it is, but it's not. Some people have to deal with stuff that is so wrong and so unfair and so unjust, and there's no way to make it right in this world. And then there are people on the other end of the spectrum, and for whatever reason, life comes unbelievably easy for them, without them doing anything obvious to deserve it. It's not fair. I'm sorry about it and I wish I could change it. I wish there were a way to hack the system, to ensure that the circumstances you are dealt in life come proportionately to your actions and goodness. But that is not the case. Life is not fair.

But here's the second phrase, and it must go in tandem with the first:

Life is good.

Life is good. I promise you, even though life is not fair, life is very, very good. In the long run, the reality that life is good outweighs the reality that life is not fair. In the short run, it doesn't always feel that way. But in the big picture, the goodness of what it means to be humans, alive and breathing on this earth, engaging with a Creator who calls us Beloved... it matters infinitely more than the fairness of circumstance.

We've got to keep both of these things in mind as we look at our shame. These statements have become vital for me, so that I can look the hard, unjust things in the face and remember the bigger picture. When our shame triggers are hit and we are trying to make sense of what is going on inside of us, when we feel like we have been wronged or like life has dealt us a bad hand, we can turn a dark corner and find that we are looking at life through a lens of shame.

The more shame, the more brokenness, the more struggle that

we deal with, the more shame becomes our lens on life. It becomes the way that we see the world, the way that we see relationships, the way that we see others, the way we see ourselves.

Families that are impacted by shame end up giving messages to each other that say things like:

"You don't have the right to be yourself."

"You don't have the right to share your pain."

"You don't have the right to heal or to become whole."

And sometimes, when people do try to share their pain, they get "should" messages.

"You shouldn't say that."

"You shouldn't do that."

"You shouldn't be that."

Shame becomes the lens on life. And it is immeasurably destructive.

The more we struggle with our shame, the more powerful it becomes. It impacts every relationship we have and everything we try to accomplish. It becomes our lens on life, the way we make sense of the world.

Life is not fair. But life is good. And shame does not need to be the lens through which we see this life.

Continue along with me, and we will walk toward grace.

A Prayer

Whew! We did it! We talked about shame, we looked at it right in the face. Wherever you are on the path to readiness, I hope the words and stories in this chapter helped you take a few more steps toward healing. We're not quite done yet talking about shame. We have to take a closer look at how it impacts our relationships. Before we do, let's pray over what we have studied together.

> *Jesus, we come to you with hearts that are vulnerable.*
> *As we begin to understand this concept of shame, we*
> *begin to see how it has held us captive and spoken lies*
> *about our worth as your children. And though we*
> *might not be ready in this very moment to understand*
> *everything you want to teach us about our shame, we*
> *are ready enough to take the next step toward healing.*
> *Will you help us to notice our shame triggers, and what*
> *they tell us about ourselves and the world? Will you*
> *help us to see when we dump the contents of our shame*
> *backpacks on the ones who love us most? Will you help*

us to believe that although life is not fair, that it is good? Will you help us shift our lens on life, from a lens of shame to a lens of grace? We trust you with this process, and we honor you in it. We will give you the glory for every step of our healing. Amen.

CHAPTER THREE

Shame in Relationships

Remember what we said in the very beginning about our references to shame: *shame is a construct*. It's a *way of thinking and talking* about the places of brokenness in our lives. It becomes a way of life. Now that we have a basic understanding of shame, we have to expand and look to our closest relationships, because our closest relationships are typically the places where we experience the most brokenness. I like to think of this part of the work like building a bridge. We build the bridge from our own shame and into our key relationships, because we're not on an island. We're not just people, alone. We are in all kinds of relationships. We're husbands, we're wives, we're significant others, we're dads, we're moms, we're bosses, we're employees, we're partners, we're friends. We have all these relationships at church, and at work, and in the world, and the reality is that shame is present in those relationships. Yep, all of them. It's true.

Shame shows up in every single one of our key relationships.

Spiritual Foundation: Ruptured from the Beginning

Shame has been a part of all human relationships since the very beginning of our existence. Adam and Eve, Cain and Abel, Moses, David ... the Bible gives us a plethora of stories to explore the work of shame in our interpersonal connections. In the Garden of Eden, the serpent used *shame* to draw Adam and Eve into making sinful choices that would begin a whole spiral of shame, lasting for countless generations. We have been ruptured from the beginning, and we cannot escape the experience of shame in our relationships. But as we study the way that brokenness as shame has influenced our becoming, perhaps we can also learn the healing power of grace.

Jesus' parable of the prodigal son certainly demonstrates this. You may remember the story of the son who asks his father to receive his inheritance early, only to go squander it away in waste and excess. Imagine the shame that entered that relationship, and the family relationships that were impacted by it. Let's look at Luke 15:11-32 in The Message:

> *Then he said, "There was once a man who had two sons. The younger said to his father, 'Father, I want right now what's coming to me.'*

"So the father divided the property between them. It wasn't long before the younger son packed his bags and left for a distant country. There, undisciplined and dissipated, he wasted everything he had. After he had gone through all his money, there was a bad famine all through that country and he began to hurt. He signed on with a citizen there who assigned him to his fields to slop the pigs. He was so hungry he would have eaten the corn-cobs in the pig slop, but no one would give him any.

"That brought him to his senses. He said, 'All those farmhands working for my father sit down to three meals a day, and here I am starving to death. I'm going back to my father. I'll say to him, Father, I've sinned against God, I've sinned before you; I don't deserve to be called your son. Take me on as a hired hand.' He got right up and went home to his father.

"When he was still a long way off, his father saw him. His heart pounding, he ran out, embraced him, and kissed him. The son started his speech: 'Father, I've sinned against God, I've sinned before you; I don't

deserve to be called your son ever again.'

"But the father wasn't listening. He was calling to the servants, 'Quick. Bring a clean set of clothes and dress him. Put the family ring on his finger and sandals on his feet. Then get a prize-winning heifer and roast it. We're going to feast! We're going to have a wonderful time! My son is here—given up for dead and now alive! Given up for lost and now found!' And they began to have a wonderful time.

"All this time his older son was out in the field. When the day's work was done he came in. As he approached the house, he heard the music and dancing. Calling over one of the houseboys, he asked what was going on. He told him, 'Your brother came home. Your father has ordered a feast—barbecued beef!—because he has him home safe and sound.'

"The older brother stomped off in an angry sulk and refused to join in. His father came out and tried to talk to him, but he wouldn't listen. The son said, 'Look how many years I've stayed here serving you, never giving you one moment of grief, but have you ever thrown a

*party for me and my friends? Then this son of yours
who has thrown away your money on whores shows up
and you go all out with a feast!'*

*"His father said, 'Son, you don't understand. You're
with me all the time, and everything that is mine is
yours—but this is a wonderful time, and we had to
celebrate. This brother of yours was dead, and he's
alive! He was lost, and he's found!'"*

Luke 15:11-32 MSG

For some of us, this parable may be a hard one. You may
relate more to the second son then the first one!

But, I love the moment in this story where the prodigal son
starts the speech he had memorized for his father, a lament of
all the shame he carried about his choices and his sin. The
father cuts him off before he is even finished! The father
throws a party and forgives the son. The crushing weight of
shame is relieved by the experience of grace. Shame entered
that relationship, and grace is what healed it.

But remember the other son? His response was hurt and
confusion. He experienced the reality that *life is not fair*, and it
caused him to be angry not only at the brother, but at the
father, too! See how the work of shame spreads, infecting our

closest relationships and causing brokenness.

We don't know the end of this story. Does the brother forgive his long-lost sibling? Does he choose to celebrate with his father? Or does he hold onto bitterness and pick up his own shame in the process.

Perhaps the important question isn't what the brother in the story does.

Perhaps the question is: *what do we do in our own story?*

When we are faced with similar situations, will we choose the bondage of shame or the freedom of grace? We will not escape being faced with these questions. We have been ruptured in relationship from the beginning. And if we have been ruptured in relationship, we can be restored in relationship. We can be empowered to choose the healing, and that is what we are invited to do.

Please note that the father never speaks a word of condemnation to the sons. The father gives both sons choices, he doesn't control or manipulate them. The father never gives up hope for change. He always waits, watches, and hopes. Also, we see that the father is openly affectionate and loving. He reconciles quickly. The father restores his son with honor and celebrates with him. God our Father longs to do the same things with us, now, today, through His grace.

A Closer Look

We've examined our own shame in the last chapter, so let's take a closer look at how it affects our relationships. The consequences of shame in our relationships can run the spectrum of damage, from trouble with communication and intimacy, all the way to total breakdown and dissolution of our relationships. As children, spouses, parents, friends, partners, co-workers, leaders, and community members, we must look at how shame is feeding into dysfunction and brokenness.

Jack and Judy Balswick were a couple of my professors at Fuller Theological Seminary when I was first beginning my learning around shame. They put a model together called the *Balswick Model of Relationships*,[14] and it was extremely eye opening to me. They taught about a graceless family and a grace-full family. Here's what they found:

In a graceless family, the dynamic looks like this:

* conditional love
* control

---

[14] Balswick, Jack and Judy. ***The Family: A Christian Perspective on the Contemporary Home***. Grand Rapids, Michigan, Baker, 1991, pp. 21-30.

- apathy
- shame

In a grace-full family, the dynamic looks like this:

- unconditional love
- empowerment
- intimacy
- grace

In their research, they found that these dynamics can span generations.[15]

Remember, we've all got shame. It already exists in our story. It already influences every relationship we have. Whether we have been raised in a grace-full family or a graceless family, we all carry our own load of shame. But for those who are on the far end of that spectrum, those who have experienced a traumatic and abusive family of origin, the wounds are so deep. A shame dynamic in a family of origin leaves profound scars and forms distorted identities. If you have come from a family like this, there is hope and healing for you. And if you came from a grace-full family, it's normal that you are still aware of some shame struggles. We all have them.

The Balswicks put it like this: "We propose a theology of family relationships which involves four sequential, but

---

[15] Balswick, Jack and Judy. Family ministry professional development training course, FY 96, 1996.

nonlinear stages: covenant, grace, empowering and intimacy. Covenant: to love and be loved. Grace: to forgive and be forgiven. Empowering: To serve and be served. Intimacy: To know and be known."[16]

It is intriguing to me how difficult it is for us to talk about our shame. We keep the most painful parts of our stories and our relationships hidden and silent. And do you know where this happens most often? The church. Don't get me wrong: I love the church. We need the church. But we also need some change in the church.

The church has to be a place where people can be real, and honest, and vulnerable. But in so many places, it's the opposite. We walk into church, dressed in our Sunday best, and when people ask us how we are, we tell them we are great! Now, of course I'm not suggesting that every time you come into church and somebody asks you how you are, that you should give them a 20-minute dissertation. The problem is that we are almost *conditioned* to respond favorably. And even when we're in other environments, like in small groups or intimate conversations with others, even then sometimes we're really hesitant to talk openly, honestly, and authentically about what's on the inside.

---

[16] Balswick, Jack and Judy. *The Family: A Christian Perspective on the Contemporary Home*. Grand Rapids, Michigan, Baker, 1991, p. 30.

This is just the beginning of how shame damages our relationships.

Shame Blocks Interpersonal Needs

We all have interpersonal needs. Especially in our close relationships, we cannot be fully healthy unless we are both giving and receiving in the ways that honor and uphold the relationship. While humans crave connection and intimacy with others, shame blocks those things because shame makes us believe that we cannot be authentic. And if we cannot be authentic, how can we even express our needs? Let alone receive what we need. We are afraid, we are closed off, and we are trying to hide the parts of ourselves that are in the *most* need for human connection.

In his outstanding book about Shame, Gershen Kaufman writes about several interpersonal needs that all humans have.[17] We have a need for **relationship** with significant others, the genuine giving and receiving of love and compassion. We have a need for **touching and holding**, to help form healthy attachments. We have a need for

---

[17] Kaufman, G. *Shame: The Psychology of shame: Theory and treatment of shame-based syndromes*. New York, Springer Publishing, 1989, p 64.

identification, which means merging with another, like in a marriage relationship. We have a need for **differentiation**, which means to separate from another, so that we do not become codependent. We have a need for **nurture**, to give and receive care and empathy. We have a need for **affirmation**, to be valued, recognized, and admired. We have a need for **power**, to have control over our own lives and decisions.

Shame blocks every single one of our interpersonal needs.

Shame turns our need for connection and attachment into unhealthy relationships. We either *over connect* and share with others, or we *under share* and keep relationships at the surface. We practice bad boundaries. We are not relational. Our shame causes us to act selfish and self-centered, destroying our relationships and preventing us from forming new, healthy ones.

Characteristics of Shame-Based Relationships

After several decades of researching and studying shame, I have identified eight key characteristics of shame-based relationships from the research. This research was influenced heavily by a list of shame systems published by Fossom and

Mason in the mid-eighties, and[18] was confirmed by my own doctoral work and subsequent research. These are the places where shame shows up in our most close and significant relationships. As you look at this list and read through the brief descriptions of each one, I invite you to think about the family you grew up in. How or where did any of these things present for you?

Characteristics of Shame Based Relationships

1. Control
2. Perfection
3. Blame
4. Denial
5. Unreliability
6. Disqualification
7. Addictions
8. Rage

No one comes into counseling saying, "I have shame. Can you help me work on that, and replace it with grace?" What people come into counseling for are the *results* of shame. When people feel like they ***are not good enough***, it manifests in one of these eight ways.

---

[18] Fossum, Merle and Mason, Marilyn. *Facing Shame: Families in Recovery*, New York, W.W. Norton and Co., 1986, pp. 86-87.

73

Shame can show itself as an abuse of **control**. If I feel ashamed, I might overcompensate and misuse power in my relationships and in my life. I might become a controller, to protect myself from being shamed.

Shame can show itself as **perfection**. If I feel ashamed, I might strive for perfection, to prove that I am indeed good enough. I create a reality where no one has a right to put me down or belittle me. The perfection becomes a cover, a way to keep everyone away from my shame.

Shame can show itself in relationship by **blame**. If I feel ashamed, it might be far easier for me to blame others, so that I can't be blamed. When I get blamed, I may feel so much shame that I can hardly handle it. The blame deflects the shame I feel.

Shame can show up as **denial**. If I feel ashamed, I may pretend there are no problems, so that I don't have to feel the shame of them. This is a way of covering the pain of being authentic and real with myself and others. The denial keeps me distant from that pain.

Shame can show itself as **unreliability**. If I feel ashamed, I may not be able to show up consistently because I am too insecure and broken. I might be undependable: hot and cold, up and down. My lack of follow through shows up because of my shame.

Shame can show up as **disqualification.** If I feel ashamed, I might feel so poorly about myself that I disqualify others. I may prop myself up and put others down as a way of feeling better about myself. Shame gets in the way and the person who struggles with shame struggles to see others as equals.

Shame can show up as **rage**. When people who struggle with shame get hurt, they are deeply hurt. That hurt might turn into anger as a way of deflecting the pain of the shame. That anger can turn to rage if it isn't healthily addressed.

Shame can show up through an **addiction**. If I feel ashamed, I might hurt so deeply that I resort to numbing it in any way possible. In order to cope, in order to not feel, in order to deal with strong feelings of being *so bad*, I may become dependent on my numbing mechanisms, which turns into an addiction.

Shame is so powerful, and it shows itself in all the ways listed above. These things are what you see and experience, but the root is shame!

Let's take a closer look at the eight characteristics of shame-based relationships. This time, as you read through them in more detail, I invite you to think about both the family you grew up in, your *family of origin*, and the family you are currently a part of, your *current nuclear family*. As you think about these two family units, I would like you to decide how you would rate the amount of dysfunction regarding that particular issue on a scale of one through ten. One would mean things were/are genuinely whole and healthy regarding that specific characteristic. Ten would mean that things were/are absolutely, off-the-charts, out of control terrible regarding that issue. Doing this exercise will help you to begin to see how these unhealthy characteristics formed the shame that you still struggle with today. The goal here is not to be disloyal to the family that you grew up in, nor to the one you are currently a part of, but to be authentic about some of the places of challenge and brokenness.

Control

The first place that shame manifests itself in a relationship is the need for control. A control system communicates that *everyone in the family must play their part, fulfill their duties, and stay within the expected boundaries*. Everything in these systems must be carefully directed and ordered, and when there is a lack of control, it upsets the family. It upsets the system. It leads to fear and chaos. Control is all about the misuse of power. Some have it. Others do not. Those who have it, misuse it. Those who don't have it, get taken advantage of.

Here's the problem with control systems: they manipulate.

They use control to accomplish an agenda without acknowledging or empathizing with the people who are in the system. Control-based systems expect complete submission, and they don't like being questioned in any way. Often, in a family where control is being misused, somebody calls the shots. There's an authoritarian. This person is *in charge*, and nobody is allowed to talk back or to push back. If you do, you get shamed and pushed down hard, because you're challenging the control in the family system.

Think about your family of origin. How often did you feel bound by a system of control? Did you feel like an authoritarian figure in your family called the shots? Did you feel free to make your own choices? How about your current family? Think of your number of control dysfunction in each family from one to ten.

Perfectionism

Systems or families that struggle with perfectionism *expect everything to be flawless*. The only acceptable GPA is a 4.0. The only acceptable position on the team is a starter. The only acceptable appearance is a perfect one, without even a hair out of place. With perfectionism, everything has to be *just right*, and even then, it's still not good enough. Perfection is an illusion. Perfectionism is a ladder that never ends. It's not even attainable, and yet it becomes the gold standard of what is expected in the family.

If someone in a family struggling with perfectionism doesn't measure up, then care and love are sometimes withheld. Or least that perception is given: *if I'm not good enough, I won't be loved. I won't be cared for. I won't matter unless I can be perfect in somebody else's eyes.*

I can relate to a struggle with perfectionism. I've been in school all my life – at one point I paid them, and now they pay me, but I'm still in school after all these many years. I just switched seats, from a student to a professor. And I love it! But I can tell you that in all my years in education, I only had one semester with a perfect 4.0. I did it just to see what it felt like. And then I never did it again. Do you know what changed after that one semester of 4.0? Nothing. Absolutely nothing. Getting the 4.0 didn't suddenly make me perfect.

In high school, I played football. I also took chemistry and biology classes, and the teachers of the classes were also the football coaches. I imagined that if I ever got an A in their classes, people would just assume that I hadn't really earned it, that it was just handed to me because of my value to the football team. And that's the problem with systems of perfectionism.

You can't win.

Even if you hit the mark, systems that are based on shame

find ways to discredit it.

Think about your family of origin. How often did you feel an expectation to be perfect? How often did you feel like love would be withheld if you didn't hit the mark? How about your current nuclear family dynamic? Think of your number of perfectionism dysfunction in both categories from one to ten.

Blame

Systems that struggle with shame, struggle with blame. You've heard of the blame game. Blame says that ***when something goes wrong, it is someone's fault***. And guess who's fault it is? Not mine! So, it must have been *you*. Systems of blame refuse to take healthy responsibility and instead usually find a scapegoat or scapegoats in the family to pin the blame on. It's typical to find a "black sheep" scenario in a system like this: some person takes an extraordinary amount of blame for bad things that happen to the family. The story is told that if the "black sheep" would just adjust and conform, or get their act together, then the whole family would be fine. Everybody would love the family if old Bob or old Joyce, that black sheep, would just stop bringing everyone down.

Systems of blame can be really convenient for those who are on the finger-pointing side of the blame. It's easier to feel better about your own mistakes and shortcomings if you can just pin your losses on someone else. The more energy that goes into the blame, the more relief there is for the person doing the blaming, because they come to the place where they buy into their own story of having no responsibility in the mess.

When you're on the wrong side of a blame system, it's pretty terrible. You lose track of what really is your responsibility, because you are being saddled with far more than your fair share. Frequently, motives are assigned to you for doing what you did, so not only are you told what you did wrong, you are told why you did it. This can be a suffocating way to live and exist in a family system.

Think about your family of origin. How often did you feel blamed for things that went wrong in the family? How often do you remember someone else in your family system being blamed for what went wrong? Did you often feel like members of your family took responsibility for their own actions? Did you feel that blame was used as a way of motivating and handling you in situations? How about your current nuclear family? Think of your number of blame dysfunction in each family from one to ten.

Denial

A simple description of a denial dynamic is this: ***real feelings and real problems are not allowed***. Families who see shame in the form of denial do not know what to do with real feelings and real problems, so they build a system that pretends hard things don't happen and negative emotions are ugly. People in these sorts of families deny feeling lonely, depressed, or anxious. They deny being afraid, being needy, and being rejected. They deny that they have any problems at all. And in fact, to the public, they act like everything is just absolutely wonderful.

Spirituality and religion can play deeply into a denial dynamic. Families can get caught up in a false sort of faith that believes the power of God can not only rescue them from every trial, it can make all painful emotions disappear into some sort of spiritual bliss. These sorts of family systems push people do try harder, believe stronger, do better, so that God can alleviate whatever problems arise and whatever feelings are felt.

I want to state, for the record, that I absolutely believe Christ Jesus does have the power to deliver us from any sort of problem or circumstance. I believe that our human emotions absolutely can be comforted by the love and grace and peace and mercy of our Father God. However, our deliverance does not always come in the way we ask or the timing we desire. Frequently, we are allowed to experience the consequences of our choices and the choices of those around us. And while the comfort and peace and joy of God are real and beautiful and powerful, they *do not erase* the genuine human emotion we experience as a result of living our lives in this world.

Do you know what happens when you deny your pain over and over and over again? It doesn't stay buried for very long. It erupts like a volcano. Eventually, you cannot carry the weight of hidden pain any longer. Something will happen, and your response erupts out of all the pain you have been hiding for weeks or months or years. You explode on the people you love the most and it usually ends up pushing them far away from you. Perhaps you have experienced this personally, or perhaps you have been the target of someone who had a back-up of denied emotion. Either way, it can be incredibly painful.

Think about your family of origin. How often did you feel like your problems and your feelings weren't allowed? Did your family openly talk about their emotions, or was that a shameful topic? Did you feel spiritually pushed towards denying your negative feelings? How about your current nuclear family? Think of your number of denial dysfunction in each family from one to ten.

Unreliability

In a family where unreliability is an expression of shame, **actions and reactions cannot be counted on to be consistent**. This dynamic creates confusion, tension, and wounds. A simple greeting may provoke a warm, affectionate response one day and an explosion of anger the next. There are always unknowns about what's coming next, emotionally or relationally.

Someone who is brought up in an unreliable environment begins to believe that life is not consistent, and people are not consistent. People don't follow through and they've got emotions all over the place, so I have to be on guard all the time because I never know what's coming next. Relationships are unreliable, and I can't depend on any consistent support or care from anyone. Maybe I'm a kid and I'm waiting for a parent to pick me up at school, and the truth is I never know if I'm going to get picked up or not. I don't even know if they will remember me on any given day. If I'm being raised in an environment like that, I don't learn to trust. I learn to try and take care of myself, and to survive.

Think about your family of origin. How often did you feel like you didn't know what was coming next in your relationships? Did your family do and say what they said they were going to do and say? Did you feel trust towards your family, or did you feel like you had to take care of yourself because no one else could be counted on? How about your current nuclear family? Think of your number of unreliability dysfunction in each from one to ten.

Disqualification

I think this may be the most damaging one of all. Disqualification says, *if anyone tries to talk about the problem, they are the problem*. If anybody tries to point out what's wrong in the family, it's easier to disqualify them or discount them than it is to deal with what they're saying. This is different than denial, because denial just says the problem doesn't exist. This is different than blame, because blame is mostly focused on reassigning responsibility. This is more of a mind-game sort of situation; gaslighting, if you're familiar with that term. Disqualification makes its target feel dismissed, invalidated, and invaluable.

If the message can't be refuted, shoot the messenger. That's disqualification. Get rid of the one who's trying to say there's a problem, or who is trying to enact change that isn't wanted. Get rid of the one who is disrupting the norms that are comfortable, or who is trying to succeed beyond mediocre expectations.

I'm convinced that disqualification gets misused in so many environments and arenas that maybe we don't even think about. I know there are women reading this book right now that have been disqualified from jobs, from relationships, from opportunities. And you know the only reason you were disqualified was because of your gender, whether it was spoken to you or not. The same goes for ethnicity. I am convinced that there are people reading these words right now that have been disqualified by gender, the color of their skin, their beliefs, their background, their name, the way they talk, their religion. *This is wrong.* The act of misusing power and disqualifying someone without engaging their skills, abilities, personality, perspectives, feelings, and humanity is damaging in every way. Please let me say...I am sorry! I must acknowledge that my privilege as an educated, Christian, white man gets in the way of my ability to truly, deeply engage at times.

Behind disqualification is always shame and fear.

Think about your family of origin. How often did you feel dismissed, invalidated, and invaluable? Did your family dismiss your perspectives and disqualify you from having opinions? Was your voice welcomed and considered, or was it disqualified? How about your current nuclear family? Think of your number of disqualification dysfunction in each family from one to ten.

Addiction

People can also allow addictions to be the expression of their shame, and this can wreak havoc on a family. Whatever the addiction is, be it alcohol, drugs, pornography, shopping, exercise, gaming, eating, or something else, the message is this: *life is too painful, and the only way to make it through is to numb and distract so that I don't have to feel the pain and shame anymore*. Behind addictions, there is always a hidden place of fear and brokenness and shame. When the addiction endorphins take over, the pain and loneliness and brokenness go numb.

You probably already know why this destroys relationships: it numbs all the good things too. Addiction draws all of our attention and our energy and our movement towards the object of our relief, and in doing so it robs us of energy for anyone and anything else. We can't feel the love we once felt, we can't find the grace and mercy we once found, we can't rally the relational bandwidth to maintain our most important connections. Addiction pulls us deeper and deeper in, leaving everything and everyone else further and further away.

VanVonderen puts it this way: "Addiction is simply the end of a course of action designed to fill inner spiritual emptiness with something that can't fill it. It is the result of an attempt to meet inner needs with external substances or activities."[19]

Think about your family of origin. Were there addictions? Maybe you didn't find out until years later that somebody

---

[19] VanVonderen, J. *Tired of Trying to Measure Up*. Minneapolis, Bethany House Publishers, 1989, p. 67.

struggled with some kind of addiction, and it now explains why there was a disconnection you didn't understand. Or maybe you saw the effects of the addiction firsthand. How about your current nuclear family? Think of your number of addiction dysfunction in each family from one to ten.

Rage

I define rage as ***out of control anger***. Let's think about this really carefully. I'm not talking about anger. Anger is a valid feeling, and normal expressions of anger are good and healthy and biblical. But when the anger gets out of control, that's when it becomes rage. Rage creates distance and causes fear. As rage outbursts become common, they cause a lack of trust.

Rage is the person who yells and shouts in your face. Rage is an expression like road rage, when someone cuts you off in traffic, follows you too close, or communicates at you with their fingers out the window. Rage is a parent screaming at their child over an innocent mistake. Rage is the silent, burning, white hot, feel and look on the face of a man in relationship with a woman, in response to something that went wrong. Rage is *searing*, and so damaging to relationships.

Think about your family of origin. How often did expression of anger seem out of control? Did you feel fear when someone in your family displayed anger? Did you feel a lack of trust due to expressions of rage? How about your current nuclear family? Think of your number of rage dysfunction in both cases from one to ten.

Your Own Shame Expressions

Control. Perfectionism. Blame. Denial. Unreliability. Disqualification. Addictions. Rage.

Alright. Take a deep breath. We've taken a closer look at these eight different characteristics of shame-based relationships, and I'm certain that at least one or two of these really connected with you. I'm certain of it because these relational dynamics happen in families and relationships all the time. It's hard to dig deeply into these spaces, especially if you've really experienced some trauma or wounds. But we're not going to stay stuck in the pain. We're going to move into the grace.

Before we move on, I'd like you to take a moment and draw what shame looks like to you. I frequently ask my students to do this, and they come up with all sorts of different imagery. Chains. Clouds. Darkness. Think about what shame looks like and feels like *to you*, and then draw it. This exercise will help you crystallize in your mind the brokenness that is ready to be healed.

I've challenged you to think a little bit about the family you grew up in as you scored your experience in each of these areas. If you scored a seven or above in any category, I would invite you to consider that there is some more work that could be done around those areas of your past. Your personal shame and brokenness are highly influenced by your experiences in your family of origin, and there is healing and wholeness that can be found as you engage these places. I recommend the help of a loving friend, a pastor, or a professional counselor.

No matter what number you scored in these areas, let's close this section with this: I want you to think about the family you're in right now. I want you to think about your current relationships: your husband, your wife, your kids, your best friends, your closest co-workers. If you scored highly in any of those areas of control, perfectionism, blame, denial, unreliability, disqualification, addiction, or rage, and you haven't done much work in that area, guess what? *It's going to show up today in your current relationships*.

As it shows up today, you're going to need to take some responsibility for that. Taking that responsibility is the path towards healing. So, here's what I want you to remember: *without some conscious work and choices, you will either repeat the patterns from the past or you will rebel against them*. Both are unhealthy.

Where are you repeating or repelling behaviors in your key relationships?

Sometimes we see that anger and rage from our family of origin, and we declare – either out loud or unconsciously – "I'm never going to be that rageful person my mom was". But now you've done a 180, and you don't get angry when you really ought to get angry over something. You either become exactly like your mom, or you rebel and do exactly the opposite. And here's the bad news: whether we repeat the pattern or we rebel against it, both places are unhealthy.

Guess where the health is? It's in the middle.

Guess where the hardest place to get to is? The middle.

I hope that for your own personal process and work, there's at least one or two of these areas where you can say that you could use some help and health in. The truth is that while the middle is hard to find, there is freedom and healing and wholeness available to you in that middle place, and God will help you to find it. His restoration work will draw you toward these places of health, as you are ready to walk towards them.

A Prayer

This is a hard conversation. It's one thing to look back and see how these shame dynamics influenced you in the past, but it's another to see them playing out in your current life and relationships. And yet, the first step is awareness; it's being open and honest about those places of brokenness and fear and shame that every one of us have. And after we're aware of it, as we are honest with those places, we can then invite God to help us make some sense of it all, and to help us find a path forward. I'll leave you with a prayer, and trust that God will meet you right where you are.

Our Good Heavenly Father, as we look at these characteristics of shame, will you make it clear to us what we need to address in our own lives? If there's something we need to take a hard look at, help us to take a look at it, even though it's painful. Help us to find some ways to deal with these places in our current relationships, and bring healing to some of these hurts from the past. Help us to get healthier in these areas so that we don't just either repeat the patterns or rebel against them. Right now, we ask you for breakthrough. We ask you to walk alongside of us. And as we do, and as you do that with us, we'll give you the praise for our healing and restoration. In your powerful name we pray, Amen.

CHAPTER FOUR

Healing for Shame

You're probably about ready for some healing after that last chapter! It is a heavy experience to look at those different characteristics of shame and to think honestly and seriously about our own backgrounds and the way these things play out in our lives and relationships. I commend your courage to journey this far into your own shame narratives and experiences. The good news is that we are going to continue on from here into some joyful and beautiful news that can mean transformation for your life and relationships. Healing for shame is possible, and it is waiting for you.

Spiritual Foundations: The Great Reversal

As we think about healing for our shame, we've got to really make a distinction between our part and God's part. What work is our responsibility, and what healing can only come from him? In order to ground ourselves in that distinction, let's look to the words and actions of Jesus in Matthew 19:

> *One day children were brought to Jesus in the hope that*

he would lay hands on them and pray over them. The disciples shooed them off. But Jesus intervened: "Let the children alone, don't prevent them from coming to me. God's kingdom is made up of people like these." After laying hands on them, he left.

Another day, a man stopped Jesus and asked, "Teacher, what good thing must I do to get eternal life?"

Jesus said, "Why do you question me about what's good? God is the One who is good. If you want to enter the life of God, just do what he tells you."

The man asked, "What in particular?"

Jesus said, "Don't murder, don't commit adultery, don't steal, don't lie, honor your father and mother, and love your neighbor as you do yourself."

The young man said, "I've done all that. What's left?"

"If you want to give it all you've got," Jesus replied, "go sell your possessions; give everything to the poor. All your wealth will then be in heaven. Then come follow me."

That was the last thing the young man expected to hear. And so, crestfallen, he walked away. He was holding on tight to a lot of things, and he couldn't bear to let go.

As he watched him go, Jesus told his disciples, "Do you have any idea how difficult it is for the rich to enter God's kingdom? Let me tell you, it's easier to gallop a camel through a needle's eye than for the rich to enter God's kingdom."

The disciples were staggered. "Then who has any chance at all?"

Jesus looked hard at them and said, "No chance at all if you think you can pull it off yourself. Every chance in the world if you trust God to do it."

Matthew 19:13-26 MSG

When I teach on this passage, I think it's really important to give the context of Jesus and the children before we read the story of the wealthy young man who wanted to get into the kingdom of heaven.

There's something unique going on here. This context matters. I picture Jesus, hanging out with the kids. He's probably down in the dirt, on his knees in the sand, playing with these children. And while he's doing that, his disciples are shooing the kids away as if they are a bother. They feel like Jesus has more important things to do than be pestered with children.

But Jesus doesn't see it that way. Kids are honest. They're authentic. They don't have agendas. When Jesus was around the adults, they always had an agenda. They were trying to trap him, to get him to say the wrong thing or do the wrong thing. I think these kids must have felt like a little respite for him. And then, of course, he used it as a teaching moment to set the stage for so many other things he had to teach his followers.

Then the passage transitions to an adult who had an agenda for Jesus. The young man stops Jesus and asks what he must do to get eternal life. His perspective is revolving solely around himself. *What must I do to receive eternal life? What's in this for me?* There's no context of relationship with Jesus. It seems like he doesn't really even need Jesus, because his questions revolve around what he himself must do in order to achieve this outcome of eternal life.

Jesus, in his compassion and wisdom, chooses to walk through this line of questioning with the man. He responds by listing off several of the 10 commandments: don't murder. Don't commit adultery. Don't steal. Don't lie. Honor your father and mother. Love your neighbor as you do yourself.

Jesus doesn't list all 10 of the commandments, but he lists the six that have to do with relationships between *humans*. He doesn't even get to the ones that have to do with the relationship between humans and God. I think he did that on purpose.

So, the young man says, "I've done all that. What's left?"

It's interesting that he had a "perfect relationship" with everyone in his life. In all my years of counseling and education, I've never come across such a perfect person. But Jesus doesn't argue the point. He simply shares the next step of the process: sell everything you have, give it to the poor, and follow me.

I think what Jesus did here was to roll all four of the other commandments that have to do with right relationship between us and God into one to-do list for this guy. The guy wanted a to-do list, so he gave him one, and it was a hefty one. The poor fellow couldn't fathom such a sacrifice, so he turned and walked away from Jesus.

And then Jesus says this: "Do you have any idea how difficult it is for the rich to enter God's kingdom? Let me tell you, it's easier to gallop a camel through a needle's eye than for the rich to enter God's kingdom."

When Jesus said that, he blew the socks off those disciples.

Well, I guess they didn't wear socks, so maybe he blew their sandals off. I picture their mouths dropped open in shock. The understanding of their whole culture was that people who were rich have God's blessing, but Jesus was saying exactly the opposite. Jesus was saying that everything about God's blessing has to do with right relationships, and not with worldly possessions and status.

The disciples were staggered. Then who has any chance at all? How could this make sense?

This is a really sobering moment for the disciples as they pause to consider the implications of Jesus' words. But Jesus' next statement gives the clarity to this seemingly impossible question. He said, "No chance at all if you think you could pull it off yourself. *Every chance in the world if you trust God to do it.*"

There's a spiritual component to this that we can't get away from in the process of dealing with our shame and our fear and our places of brokenness.

Our part is to engage with our shame, to be honest and transparent about our brokenness, and to trust and lean into relationship with the God who heals all things. As that relationship flourishes, healing deepens.

God's part is to do the healing.

What do you think one of the hardest things ever is for people who have been hurt and broken by fear and shame? *Trust.* We don't trust people because we've been hurt by people. We've been betrayed and we've been taken advantage of, we've been left by the side of the road and our hearts have been broken. We don't entrust our lives or our hearts to anyone, anymore. We take care of ourselves. We're survivors.

And maybe that's what is going on for this guy who came to Christ. Maybe that was his agenda, to figure out how to do this thing himself, because he believed he was the only one who could.

Ultimately, God does the heavy lifting when it comes to healing. Our part mostly has to do with learning what it means to trust something outside of ourselves. And for some of us, that's a really challenging thing to do.

Coming Alongside

A number of years ago, the world of basketball fandom witnessed a young girl who was rescued from a shame story.

13-year-old Natalie Gilbert had won the right to sing the national anthem on national TV before a playoff game at the Moda Center, featuring the Portland Trailblazers. She prepared for the big day with plenty of practice. As she walked out onto the stage she was beautifully dressed and truly captivated the crowd.

22,000 people in the stadium joined people everywhere watching on ESPN, and all eyes were on her. She stepped forward to sing the national anthem, and stage fright took over. She forgot the words; nothing came out. It was every performer's worst nightmare!

As she stood there in a frozen panic, Maurice Cheeks, the coach of the Trail Blazers, came over to her. He put his hand on her shoulder and he started singing the words to the national anthem. And, just for the record, he cannot sing!

Immediately, the tension relaxed. Everyone in the stadium began to smile. Natalie looked at Coach Cheeks, and then she started singing along with him, and as they sang the song together the crowd went nuts. The footage of this rescue played everywhere. *SportsCenter* picked it up. Then *Good Morning America*. The kid turned into a celebrity for at least 15 minutes. All because someone chose to come alongside her.[20]

---

[20] Deveny, Shawn. "Hall of Famer Maurice Cheeks recalls national anthem assist: 'I didn't know I would do that'". https://

Later, in an interview, she said, "What started out to be the worst moment of my life, turned out to be the best!"[21]

Can you imagine what it might have been like for her in that moment? National television, in front of thousands of people. Imagine the humiliation she must have felt, and then imagine the relief when the moment was redeemed. That shame story that could have attached to her for the rest of her life was changed by a guy who stepped over and started singing, even when he couldn't sing.

Sometimes we have the illusion that if we're going to help other people, we've got to be perfect. We've got to have all our stuff together, and we can't have any problems. But that's not true. Sometimes the presence of someone in our lives makes all the difference in the world, even when they're a broken person, too. There's power in connection.

Part of the power and redemption of shame is connecting with somebody else who comes alongside and makes a difference in our life. A lot of times, it looks like Christ: kindness, empathy, mercy. Maybe it doesn't always have a spiritual dimension to it outwardly, but there's something

---

www.sportingnews.com/us/nba/news/maurice-mo-cheeks-national-anthem-natalie-gilbert-video-coach-nba-hall-of-fame-trail-blazers/h749s8eomo4l1gy86ju2g9r26. Accessed 28 June 2021.

[21] Muldoon, Katy. "Dizzying Freeze Fame." *Oregonian,* 2003.

powerful in that sort of compassionate movement towards another person.

I call it grace.

Grace is a connection, a moment, a breakthrough that brings redemption to a place of shame. And it is a spiritual experience!

And with that, I hope you begin to feel the tug of hope.

The Key to Healing Shame

Brené Brown is very well-known in the area of shame. She's done more research and writing about it than anyone else out there. Her work seemingly is not targeted to any Christian or religious market, but I find it intriguing and affirming to read what she writes about the impact of spirituality on shame.

> *Spirituality is recognizing and celebrating that we are all inextricably connected to each other by a power greater than all of us, and that our connection to that power and to one another is grounded in love and compassion. Practicing spirituality brings a sense of*

perspective, meaning and purpose to our lives.[22]

Did you catch that?

A person who does extensive research and counseling, without a spiritual agenda, believes that spirituality is vital in our healing around shame!

When I teach this, I always ask people to draw a picture of grace, just like we drew a picture of shame. I tell them to draw some image that represents grace to them, this movement of compassion that redeems an experience of shame. Some people draw doves. Some people think about water - the ocean, or waterfalls. Some people draw pictures of Christ. Some draw hands, some draw diagrams of people connected in intimacy with each other. Think for a moment about what image comes to your mind when you think about grace.

Maybe you'll also want to write out your own definition of grace. What does grace mean to you?

You might remember the old song, *What if God Was One of Us?*, by Joan Osborne. When I'm trying to conjure a picture of grace, or a definition of grace, I often think of these words.

---

[22] Brown, Brené. *The Gifts of Imperfection*. Minneapolis, MN, Hazelden Information & Educational Services, 2010, p. 64.

If God had a name what would it be?
And would you call it to his face?
If you were faced with Him in all His glory
What would you ask if you had just one question?

What if God was one of us?
Just a slob like one of us
Just a stranger on the bus
Tryin' to make his way home?

If God had a face what would it look like?
And would you want to see if, seeing meant
That you would have to believe in things like heaven
And in Jesus and the saints, and all the prophets?

What if God was one of us?
Just a slob like one of us
Just a stranger on the bus
Tryin' to make his way home?[23]

I've got good news. God *is* one of us. He sent his son Jesus here as a representative to say, "I get it." He lived 33 years on this earth, and he figured out what it was like to deal with all

---

[23] Osborne, Joan. "One of Us." *Relish*, Mercury, 1995.

this stuff that we have to deal with. He was shamed. He knows what it's like to carry shame.

So, when we come to him with our brokenness and fear and shame, guess what?

He gets it, because He lived it.

What if that's our picture of grace? Empathy to the maximum expression. What if grace means that you have a spiritual connection to someone who _gets what it's like to be broken_? He gets what it's like to be betrayed, left alone, hurt, despised, beaten. He gets the experience of dysfunctional families and He can relate to your story. He cares deeply about the process and healing of that and wants to offer that to us.

The Johari Window

The Johari Window[24] is a technique that helps people better understand their relationship with themselves and others. It was created by psychologists Joseph Luft and Harrington Ingham in 1955 and has remained an excellent tool for self-evaluation and awareness. It helps us to model ourselves in

[24] Dinesh, Soni. _An Introduction to Johari Window_. 2019 Kindle edition.

relationship with other people so that we can find places of health and unhealth.

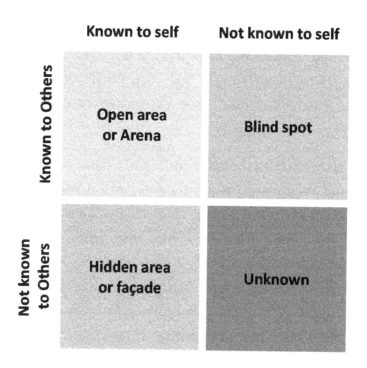

The Johari Window Model

The Johari Window has four different boxes: the open box, the blind box, the hidden box, and the unknown box.

The first box is called the open box. *The open box contains material about you that is known to yourself and known to others*. Think about the things people know about you – your background, your likes and dislikes, your attitude in any given situation, your voiced perspectives. For instance, after reading this far you know a lot of open information about me. You know that I've lived in Oregon for about 30 years and I teach at George Fox University. You know that I love the Oregon Coast and football. You know that I'm married and that I've got a couple of grown kids. You know that this material is really important to me. This is all open information, so it would go in the open box.

The second box is called the blind box. *The blind box contains material about yourself that is not known to you, but known to others*. It's things that are true about me that I am not aware of, but other people can see. For example, there are things I am not aware of about myself that my wife sees clearly, since she's been with me for over 30 years. Sometimes she shares those things with me in loving and graceful ways; she points something out about my snoring or my other particular behaviors, like my sunflower seed eating and ice chewing, that she doesn't appreciate. Those are just silly things, but you get the idea.

Sometimes, relationally and emotionally, the blind box contains things that are far more important than ice and sunflower seeds. I do things that I'm really unaware of. Some of those things are good, and some of them can be damaging. Other people can see those things in me even when I can't see them in myself. We *all* have blindness, places where we can't see things in ourselves. And I think God built us that way on purpose.

Now, if someone points those things out to me, they aren't blind anymore. They transfer from the blind box to the open box, because someone has made me aware of something in the blind box. And this is a good thing! We will always be healthier in community. God made us relational beings. In a safe environment, our community actually comes alongside of us, helping to make us aware of our blind spots and therefore making us healthier.

Third box is called the hidden box. *The hidden box contains material about yourself that is known to you, but not known to others*. These are the things that I know about myself, but I work really, really hard to make sure no one else discovers them. You know why? Fear and brokenness and shame. Part of me is afraid that if you really knew who I was, if you knew all the things that I hide, you wouldn't love me. You wouldn't trust me, you wouldn't read my book. If I had started out by sharing all the mistakes I've made, all the defeats I've had, all the temptations I've fought … You might just think of me as a total mess.

We all have a hidden box. We all work to keep some things hidden, to preserve our image and credibility, to put our best foot forward, to deny our own places of shame. Fear and embarrassment keep that stuff hidden, pushed down because we're afraid of what happens if we're really authentic and honest with each other.

A number of years ago, I did some counseling with a couple. Let's call them Lew and Doris. Lew was a tough guy. He was built short and stocky, like a fighter, and he was just angry. He made it very obvious that he didn't want to be in counseling, that he thought it was a waste of time and money. His wife, Doris, was a nurse. She was helper, full of empathy and care, and she wanted to be there to work on their marriage.

Each time we would meet, Doris would start crying almost immediately after my first comment or question. We would have therapy sessions for 50 minutes, and she would cry, and he would refuse to engage. It was really difficult therapy. We got nowhere. I did everything I knew to do. When my techniques weren't getting us anywhere, I went for help to my supervising counselor. I read books. I tried new approaches. Nothing was working.

After about six months of marital therapy, they came in one week and said, basically, "Thanks, but no thanks. This was really a waste of our time and money, and not helpful in any way."

And the truth is, part of me said, "Good! Sadly, I don't know what else to do!" And the other part of me was really sad. Honestly, I was not helpful to them, and that was a really challenging reality for me. It was one of those moments that caused me to question my own skills and abilities as a counselor, even my choice to remain in this line of work.

About a year later, I got a phone call from the husband. He sounded a lot different than he had in counseling. The first thing he said was, "Hi, this is Lew. You may not remember me."

"Ha!" I thought, "Oh, trust me. I remember you." I answered with something a bit more professional.

He told me that he needed to come back in to see me, so we set up an appointment. When he arrived, Lew didn't make eye contact with me at first. He walked into the room, sat down, fumbled with his keys for a while, and then finally looked at me. Something was very different. He was not defiant, not angry. There was a humble look in his eyes.

Before I could even begin with the pleasantries, he launched into something that he had prepared to say to me. "Dr. Shaw, thank you for seeing me today. I came here because I need to ask for your forgiveness."

Well, that certainly got my attention.

He said, "When I was in counseling with my wife before, when we were here, I was involved in an active affair. Every question and comment from you and Doris just triggered my fear and shame. I couldn't answer, because I was hiding the situation that I was dealing with. I couldn't be honest about anything. My mind was on overload, because I was trying to figure out how to answer your questions without giving away what was really going on. The lies were building on each other, and I was afraid she would put the pieces together. I knew eventually somebody would figure out that I was being unfaithful."

Then he said, "I was sabotaging the counseling. But my affair is known now. I'm making amends with everybody that I need to say I'm sorry to. I don't know if my marriage is going to make it, but I'm doing what I feel like I need to do. And I need to ask for your forgiveness for the way I treated you in counseling."

I invited him to tell me more of the story, and we talked for hour. When he left, he cried and we hugged and prayed, and then I never saw him again. I don't know the rest of his story, but what I know is that the hidden parts of his life were destroying his relationships. Those hidden places had all kinds of ramifications that he finally had to deal with.

We all have hidden places that we're managing and that we don't let people into, even if our stories are not as dramatic as Lew's story. We're afraid of what our wives, our husbands, our best friends, our pastors, our teachers, our bosses, our employees will think or feel or want or need if we're really honest with them. And the truth is, some of us have probably been authentic and honest with some of those hidden places, and then experienced the pain of it not going very well. And maybe we learned, *don't do that again*. If we share the hidden box with people that aren't safe, we can get a pretty devastating response that only reinforces the shame narratives we carry about ourselves.

The last box is the unknown box. It's my favorite. I call it the science fiction box, the Star Trek box. ***The unknown box contains material about yourself that is not known to you or to others***. It mostly contains material about the self that is unconscious material. Why we do and don't do things. Intentions. Desires. Deep places that we don't access without lots of reflection, therapy, personal work and understanding. That's why I call it the sci-fi box. It stretches the mind a little bit to contemplate how one can know that truth exists but is not known to anyone. If *no one* knows a truth, then can that truth still exist? Especially if that truth is about *you*?

Let me give you an example.

There are lots of experiences in life that are unknowns. Things that we have never encountered, places where we simply don't know how we will feel or react because we don't have any data to make an accurate prediction. We might look forward to those experiences, but we also might fear them.

They are unknown.

Freud talked about unknowns as the unconscious. You've heard of the iceberg example, right? Freud believed that the mind is like an iceberg.[25] All we ever see of an iceberg is just the little peak that's above the water, but the massive part of the iceberg is below the surface. The conscious parts of our brains are like the small peaks above the water. The unconscious parts, the icebergs underwater, actually make up the vast majority of our brain, and all of that brain power belongs in the unknown box. This involves our unknown intentions, the hidden reasons why we do things or don't do things, the driving forces within us that we are not aware of. The unknown box plays a significant role in who we are.

Open, blind, hidden, and unknown.

As you work towards being the healthiest version of yourself, you want your open box to be the biggest box. An ever-expanding open box means an ever-rising trajectory of growth and health. The more you are aware of, and the more you allow others to be aware of, the more you can consciously choose healthy behaviors and relationships, and the less shame you will carry.

---

[25] McLeod, S. A. (2015). *Unconscious Mind*. Simply Psychology. https://www.simplypsychology.org/unconscious-mind.html. Accessed 28 June 2021.

The blind box grows smaller as you move towards health, because you want to become aware of your blind spots. There will always be some things that you can't see about yourself, but that your community can. When you're rooted in a safe and caring and loving community, they participate in your growth. They come alongside you to help bring blind places out into the open.

The hidden box shrinks as you choose to release your places of shame into a safe community. This is good and healthy. The more we release from the hidden box, the less power that fear and brokenness and shame have over us. However, there will *always be some hidden stuff*. And this is good. We call it **boundaries**. Not everyone in your life needs to know about all of your dirt and grime. Not everyone needs access to your most vulnerable stories and your places of weakness. We choose *safe, appropriate, and helpful people* to open those spaces to, but we'll always have to manage some hidden stuff.

And lastly, 'til the day we die, we will have some unknown places. Until we get to what's beyond, there is unknown territory to chart.

To quantify a healthy Johari Box in some way, let's pick a number. If there were 100 parts of a person, a healthy person would have maybe 75 parts in the open box. Maybe 10 parts would be in the blind box, waiting for others to discover and share. Maybe another 10 parts would be in the hidden box, where boundaries are purposely in place. And maybe five parts would be in the unknown box, waiting to be discovered. That's kind of a healthy picture, and as we grow and change, those parts move from different boxes to the open box.

Moving Toward Health

When we use the Johari Box to assess our health, we talk about health occurring when pieces move into the open box. Every time a piece of you moves into the open box, you get a little healthier. However, the move from the blind box, the hidden box, or the unknown box into the open box is frequently painful. That's an important thing to remember as we work to redeem our shame. That pain is *health*. It is growth. But it is almost always painful.

Curt Thompson describes the experience of what happens when we expand the open box of our own Johari windows. "If you allow yourself to be known by God, you invite a different, frankly terrifying experience. You are now in a position of vulnerability. In essence, you must trust another with yourself ...to be known means that you allow your shame and guilt to be exposed in order for them to be healed."[26]

When Lew acknowledged that he was in an affair, he moved a pretty huge thing from the hidden box to the open box. He brought that shameful hiding to a close and began to deal with the consequences of his choices in order to heal himself and his marriage. I'll bet that hurt a lot. It was probably the most painful experience of his life to admit those things to his family, his church, his community. It may have caused the loss of his marriage, his kids, his friends. He may have had other consequences to experience. It's incredibly painful to experience that sort of illumination of a secret.

And yet, in the long run, he got healthier. His shame began to be relieved the moment he started telling people the truth. I could see the growth and health in him when he came to apologize to me, and when he told me of all the other places where he was seeking forgiveness. The burden of secrecy and lies was lifted, and grace could start to do its healing work in his life. It's so important to remember that health and growth often have a component of pain.

In the long run, it's healthy. In the short run, it hurts.

---

[26] Thompson, Curt. *Anatomy of the Soul: Surprising Connections between Neuroscience and Spiritual Practices That Can Transform Your Life and Relationships*. Carrollton, TX, Tyndale, 2010, p. 23.

As we move toward grace and breakthrough and healing, let's expect there to be pain involved in the process.

It may not even feel like we're getting healthier in the short run. We may have to remind ourselves that pain is health, especially in work around shame. We need support as we do this work, we need a community that will come alongside of us and engage this pain with grace. We need friends who will sing the words when we forget them. Ultimately, we have God with us as we journey. And his grace is enough.

A Prayer

I hope you are beginning to feel some hope in relation to shame. As you become conscious of the ways to release your hidden places and embrace your blind spots, you also become more open to receiving the grace of God. That grace comes from his voice, speaking to you in the deep and intimate places of your heart. And it also comes to you from his people, who choose to meet your shame and fear and weakness with compassion, empathy, mercy, and love. Before we move on, let's pray together.

God, our Creator and Sustainer, thank you that you

don't leave us alone in our process of healing. Thank you that you understand what it's like to go through what we go through here. Thank you that even through pain, you can produce health and growth and change. Thank you for reminding us that we don't have to heal on our own – that our part is to come to you and your part is to heal. Wherever we are in that process right now, come alongside of us and pull us forward in your perfect timing to get us exactly where you want us in our relationships now. Sing the words we have forgotten. Speak the grace our hearts are longing for. And help us to trust you in the process of it all. In your powerful name, Amen.

CHAPTER FIVE

Grace and Rest

Rest. That's a welcome word, isn't it? After all this work around shame, and digging into our pasts, and moving things from our blind boxes to our open boxes ... I think we're all ready for some real rest! We've taken the time to think about grace – what it looks like, what it feels like, and what healing it could bring to our places of shame. But grace isn't just about relief in our shame. Grace is about wholeness and flourishing and rest. It's about a way of life and love that can play out in our relationships with God and with others. How can we come to a place of rest for our souls?

Spiritual Foundations: Unforced Rhythms of Grace

One of the most important teachings of Jesus about the idea of grace is found in Matthew 11:25-30 MSG.

> *Abruptly Jesus broke into prayer: "Thank you, Father, Lord of heaven and earth. You've concealed your ways*

from sophisticates and know-it-alls, but spelled them out clearly to ordinary people. Yes, Father, that's the way you like to work."

Jesus resumed talking to the people, but now tenderly. "The Father has given me all these things to do and say. This is a unique Father-Son operation, coming out of Father and Son intimacies and knowledge. No one knows the Son the way the Father does, nor the Father the way the Son does. But I'm not keeping it to myself; I'm ready to go over it line by line with anyone willing to listen.

"Are you tired? Worn out? Burned out on religion? Come to me. Get away with me and you'll recover your life. I'll show you how to take a real rest. Walk with me and work with me—watch how I do it. Learn the unforced rhythms of grace. I won't lay anything heavy or ill-fitting on you. Keep company with me and you'll learn to live freely and lightly."

Matthew 11:25-30 MSG

The truth is, this is a tough one for me. I'm a perfectionist, a go-getter. I'm an extrovert, and I'm a do it myself kind of guy. So, when I read Jesus' words about connection with something beyond myself and settling into this rhythm of life, I have some trouble doing it. I love that *idea* of a rhythm, a sense of balance, a sense of purpose and meaning. But often, this means a rhythm that is quieter and slower than the pace I would like to keep. And it means trusting God!

As a professor at George Fox University, this is something that continues to challenge and grow me, because the University has a Quaker background. You may or may not know much about the Quakers, but their spiritual disciplines are very reflective, meditative, quiet, and humble. The reality is that it's a good discipline for me to be in an environment where I have to move outside of the way I'm wired to live life.

It is not atypical for me to sit in a meeting where we are trying to reach conclusions and make decisions and for someone to say, "Let's go ahead and just have about 30 minutes of silence, just to see if God is going to speak. We're going to take the time to reflect a little bit before we move forward with this really important thing that we're doing in the school or the department. And if God moves, and you want to say something, then we invite you to share that. If not, then I just invite you to be silent during this time."

Oh my gosh, I don't know about you, but on the inside I'm like, "30 minutes of silence?! Let's just take a nap, for crying out loud!" That's *not* how I'm wired. It is a real discipline for me to be alert and engaged and reflective during those times of silence and contemplation.

And yet, I've seen the way the Spirit works when we choose to do just that. Not only in the room, but in my own heart and life.

There are times when we have to slow down. When we purposely invite the Spirit into places where we might rush in on our own and try to figure stuff out, we end up with a lot less chaos and mistakes that we have to back and fix.

But look at what Jesus says about these unforced rhythms of grace: there is *real rest* for our souls. There is a chance to recover our lives. There is a Spirit who will walk with us and work with us, and who will teach us how to live *freely and lightly*.

This, my friends, is the way of grace.

Grace is Experienced

As we learn about how to find rest in the midst of grace, we have to remember that grace is a tangible thing to experience. It's not just a comforting word or a religious term. It's an *experience* of life that can transform us. If we only think about it in terms of how we can define it, we're engaging it only with our heads. But we can only get so close to God's rest and grace through our own cognitions. There is more to experience and discover.

I teach my students that there are three different aspects of our decision making and our personal process in life: *head, heart, and hands*. Often, these three categories of choices will present themselves in all kinds of scenarios.

Head refers to our cognition. This is our place of logic and reason, where rational thinking happens. It's where we make sense of things and make decisions about the practical data we receive.

Heart refers to our feelings. This is how we experience things in terms of emotion and internal gut reaction. It's where we process things on an experiential level and remember how they made us feel.

Hands refers to our behavior. This is our place of decision and action. It's where we choose to move forward and make changes in response to the situations we face. It's what we do.

The head, heart, and hands theory isn't original to me. The field of psychology refers to treatment in these different areas as cognitive therapy, affective therapy, and behavioral therapy. We all use all three of those areas – head, heart, and hands – but every one of us has one of those that's stronger than the other two.

So, if you're a cognitive person and you're faced with a dilemma, you use your brain, your cognition, your logic to make sense of things. If you're an affective person, you use your feelings and emotions to make sense of things and feel your way through life. If you're a behavioral person, you take action even when you aren't sure how you think or feel.

As we navigate our life and relationships, we are going to encounter people of all three types. And frequently we try and engage people based on our own terms. So, if I'm a cognitive person, I might engage others from a cognitive place, when what they really need might be a behavioral approach to the situation. We generally lean into our strongest area, and sometimes what we need is to come alongside someone and speak to them in their own language.

This is good information in general, to help us figure out how to work well with people. But in the context of grace, it's vital.

Grace must be experienced, felt, and lived.

You can only get so close to grace by putting it on paper, or thinking it through, or behaviorally dealing with it. Grace can only truly be understood on a feeling, experiential level. As we look to the source of grace, we realize that to fully understand it we must be present and active in an ongoing relationship between God and us. We must experience grace not just once, but moment to moment. We are cleansed moment to moment by grace, and we grow moment to moment through grace.

Lewis Smedes, a former professor of mine at Fuller Seminary, wrote a book a number of years ago called *Shame and Grace*. He writes that people experience God's grace in one of four ways: pardon, acceptance, power, or gratitude. As[27] we think about those experiences, we can see how they can play out in our lives.

Grace as pardon is a release of the consequences of something I've done. This goes beyond forgiveness to mercy—I committed an offense, but I am released from paying the penalty for the crime. I am forgiven and freed from my shame because the grace has bought my pardon.

Grace as acceptance is a feeling that I am enough. The grace of acceptance feels like love and connection and affirmation. If I experience grace as acceptance, then I know there is nothing I have to do to earn love and worthiness. It's like being cradled and held.

Grace as power is an energy to change and grow. The grace of power feels like approval and validation and encouragement. If I experience grace as empowerment, I feel alive and

---

[27] Smedes, Lewis. *Shame and Grace*. New York, Zondervan Publishing, 1993, pp. 108.

energized and released to become all that I am created to be.

Grace as gratitude is an overwhelming thankfulness to God. The grace of gratitude feels the blessing of the gifts of grace. If I experience grace as gratitude, I see and feel God's favor and blessing and respond in thankfulness.

Now, even if one of those doesn't jump out at you as the way you personally experience grace, can you see how any one of those experiences would be transformative and encouraging as you engage a God who wants to bring you out of shame and into grace?

The Source of Grace

In the last chapter I asked you to think about what your personal definition of grace is. Maybe you even drew a picture that represented grace to you. Think about that again as we look to the source of grace.

> *All that men receive from God is "by grace," from*
> *creation to final redemption ... grace is never*
> *impersonal or something apart from God himself. It is,*
> *rather, precisely a personal expression of God's nature*
> *(and as such spiritual and moral) that has meaning. It*

is mercy and love and patience and long-suffering,
never deserved by men, never compelled by any sort of
divine necessity, but always freely given and always
conditioned by moral considerations so far as its
reception by men is concerned.[28]

Yes! This is the beautiful gift of grace. Patience and mercy and love all put together. The source of grace is God, and I would argue that grace, most simply, *is God Himself.*

Grace is not just a quality of God, it's actually part of what it means for Him to be holy. It's part of who He is.

Grace cannot be set aside or cut off from a person, and it can't be cut off from God. Grace allows for meaningful relationships to exist and to flourish. Grace is relational. God acts as a *whole person* to *whole persons*. God does not just give a part of Himself to a part of us. He doesn't separate justice and mercy, grace and wrath; that's what we do. We make those separations because our minds can't fully comprehend the reality of grace. But God is perfect. He has all of these attributes within Him, and they work perfectly in conjunction

---

[28] Wynkoop, M.B. *A Theology of Love: The Dynamic of Wesleyanism.* Kansas City, Beacon Hill Press Publishing, 1972, p. 197.

with one another to form a God of Grace.

Cycles of Shame and Grace

I hope you are feeling the truth of God's love for you as you read these words. I hope you understand just how deeply God cares for you and wants the best for you. He's on your side. He's rooting for you in your darkest moments and most difficult circumstances. He is longing to bring you rest and grace and breakthrough.

A number of years ago, Jeff VanVonderen wrote a book called, *Tired of Trying to Measure Up*. This book was particularly formative to me as I began my own doctoral work in shame and grace. VanVonderen proposes a Rest Cycle, and this was always intriguing to me. In fact, when I published my original dissertation, I created the following diagrams that were inspired by VanVonderen's work.[29]

---

[29] VanVonderen, J. *Tired of Trying to Measure Up*. Minneapolis, Bethany House Publishers, 1989.

Dr. Richard Shaw

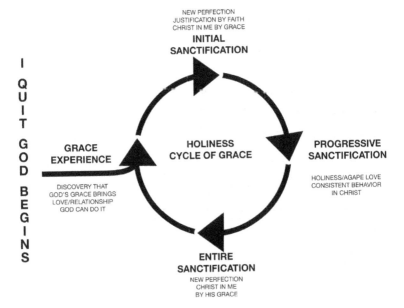

Here we have two different cycles: a cycle of shame and a cycle of grace.

Let's think about the shame cycle first. Shame always comes to a person from the outside *first*. As small children, we didn't

129

understand this introduction of shame. We didn't have power, we didn't have control, we didn't have the ability to reject messages of shame. Shame often came to us first before we even could put words to what was happening. This shame came from people who were around us that had power to shame us in some way. Unfortunately, as we have seen as we looked to our families of origin, it typically started with our closest community.

As shame comes to a person from the outside, they can get locked into the **giving up cycle**. If we believe we should be ashamed about parts of ourselves, we engage in negative behavior that substantiates our shame story. Not only that, but we find people along the way who also affirm the story. We begin to listen to people who support the idea that we ought to be ashamed, and their affirmation of that narrative embeds in our brain and in our beliefs. As we start believing the messages that people have poured into us, we accept the reality that we aren't good enough, and some of us simply give up trying to be.

As shame begins to build in our minds, we start catching and capturing all the shame that's getting poured into us. And we start believing it to be true. Out of that belief system comes negative behaviors. If I believe that I'm not worthy, how could I believe that I would do something worthy? If I believe I'm a person of shame, then I'm going to do negative, shameful things that complete the cycle and affirm the narrative. The negative behavior then leads to more messages that shame.

Eventually, in the giving up cycle, we don't even need the outside sources to shame us or affirm the narrative. We learn to do that all on our own. It doesn't take very many times of me proving to myself that I'm not worthy before I don't need outside sources to tell me anymore. At some point along the way, I conclude that the outside sources that said things about me were true, and that's the way I choose to live. I become my own worst enemy. I shame myself. And by the way, I'm much better at shaming myself than anyone else is. I know my own issues. I know my own problems. I know where to and how to beat myself up. Eventually, the giving up cycle leads to quitting.

But not everyone gets stuck in the giving up cycle, or ends up quitting. Sometimes something happens in people, a **motivating experience**, and they free themselves from the giving up cycle and move onto the **trying harder cycle**. And we start thinking, *if I would just do more, and be better, not ever make any mistakes, then maybe I wouldn't have to be ashamed of myself. If I could somehow convince myself, or convince God, that I could do all the right things, then I would be worthy of love. Maybe if I just try harder and do all the positive behaviors I can imagine, maybe I could make myself feel better and I could get rid of my own shame and **I could heal myself**.*

When we are living in the trying harder cycle, we go above and beyond to prove our worth. We do every positive behavior we can imagine, adding more and more in a seemingly endless effort to free ourselves from shame. Cheerleaders come alongside us in the trying harder cycle, too. They give messages that affirm our positive behavior. As I'm doing all kinds of good and right and appropriate things, people encourage me. They tell me I'm doing great, and that I should keep going.

We spin in this trying harder cycle where we think we're solving our own problems and dealing with our own shame. We think we're going to be fine on our own power and our own strength. And for a while, we are fine. But there are two huge problems with the trying harder cycle. Firstly, we get tired. At some point, we just can't keep up anymore, and we run ourselves ragged in the pursuit of something we can never fully find. Secondly, we don't really believe our own press. Even if we make ourselves look bright and shiny on the outside, we still know our own interior. We still feel like we are hiding our shame rather than healing it.

So, we wear ourselves out or we become frustrated with our lack of healing, and we end up in relapse, more ashamed than when we started. We go back to the giving up cycle, only this time it's worse. Now, instead of doing positive behaviors, I do negative behaviors. I do negative behaviors that affirm the message that I'm not good enough and that I should be ashamed. People come alongside to judge my failure and it hurts more this time, because they used to praise me for my success. So I spin around in this giving up cycle until I rally the strength to try again, and then I put myself right back in the trying harder cycle.

The figure eight pattern between giving up and trying harder is no way to live, and yet many people caught in shame do exactly this.

Where is the hope, then? It's coming, I promise.

Giving up and trying harder are both all about us. They are about what we can or can't do. In order to change that model, we have to find a new source, a new authority that gets to decide our value and worth. That source is God. Grace is not about my behavior. It is not about what I can do. It's about what God does on my behalf.

If you look at the diagram of the grace cycle, you'll see that it begins where we quit. When we stop the giving up and trying hard, and we welcome God's grace, everything changes. This begins with a **grace experience**, where the grace of God disrupts our shame and we begin to see that our value is truly defined by Him.

As I get in touch with that new source, and I understand that

God is there with me and for me, I begin to rest. When I see that He is on my side and it's about Him, not about me, I start to learn new messages about myself. I begin to experience the process of **sanctification**. I begin to believe that I am deeply loved, deeply accepted. I begin to receive the truth that I am forgiven, and that I am a new creation in Christ. As that process happens, I don't find myself trying hard for perfection anymore. But I also don't find myself giving up on positive behavior. Instead, the fruit of this process of rest is **consistent behavior**.

Now, here's a truth that we all need to grasp, to remember it and come back to it as often as we need to: *Consistent behavior is not perfection.*

Consistent behavior looks more like two steps forward and one step back. It's not perfection, and it's not giving up. It's an overall trajectory towards health and wholeness. People in recovery circles talk about two steps forward and one step back. At the end of the day, if you do two steps forward and one step back five times, guess what? You're five steps ahead of where you were when you started! That's awesome!

It doesn't always feel awesome, though. Every time you fall back, it's tempting to feel like you've lost everything and you're starting completely over. It's not true, but that's what it feels like. When you've been trying make progress in some area of your life, to get healing and change, and then you blow it, it feels terrible. It's so disappointing and so hard. You might feel like you want to give up.

Now, I'm a counselor. I spent a lot of time helping people with their feelings. And here's a secret I want you to remember: *sometimes, your feelings are not telling you the whole truth*. While it might feel like you are making no progress, that simply is not always the case.

Let's take this just a couple steps more.

Not only are your feelings not telling you the whole truth... your head and your hands aren't telling you the whole truth either. Just as we cannot assess our journey based only on our feelings, we also cannot assess our journey based only on our actions or only on our thoughts. It takes all three, working together, to truly get a realistic picture of our progress and growth.

When you are working towards healing, take the time to assess your thoughts, feelings, *and* actions. You will most likely see that you *have* moved forward, and that you can get up again and make more efforts to move in the right direction. Consistent behavior looks like two steps forward, even when the one step backs continue to happen. In the long run, you're headed in the right direction. And that direction is not perfection. It's rest in the truth that you are the Beloved of

God Himself.

There's a song that speaks to the truth of this rest cycle: *Rest Easy* by Audio Adrenaline. I encourage you to let these lyrics invite your heart towards grace.

> *One more mile 'til I lay rest*
> *I have put myself through this rigid test*
> *But the mile has never ended*
> *no distance has been gained*
> *I do not see greatness I wanted to obtain*
> *Where is my embrace from the race that I have run?*
> *I have kept a steady pace but still I have not won*
>
> *Rest easy*
> *have no fear*
> *I love you perfectly*
> *love drives out fear*
> *I'll take your burden*
> *you take My grace*
> *Rest easy*
> *in My embrace*
>
> *I am such a sinner I fear my evil ways*
> *I fear my imperfection I fear my final days*

I just want to take control and snap this rusty chain
drop my heavy burden it seems to be in vain

I am not a bold man even though I want to be
I am just a dreamer with a timid history
Scared of confrontations I fume all through the night
the world has its hold on me and I just want to fly
The sky, the sky is open wide
but I can't fly 'til I step aside

Rest easy
have no fear
I love you perfectly
and perfect love drives out fear
I'll take your burden
you take My grace
Rest easy in My embrace
Rest easy, rest easy, rest easy,
in My embrace
Rest easy[30]

---

[30] Audio Adrenaline. "Rest Easy." *Don't Censor Me*, Gaga Studios, 1993.

Shame Transforms Into Grace

This is one of my favorite moments in the study of shame and grace, because we get to look at how grace transforms all our expressions of shame. You probably remember the list we studied in chapter three: control, perfection, blame, denial, unreliability, disqualification, addiction and rage. That was a pretty painful list for all of us, because those things lead to the core of our shame stories.

But now is the moment for hope to really come alive in the face of all of those things. You've done the hard work of looking at those expressions of shame in your life, both in your family of origin and in your current family unit. Now, I want you to see the change that can happen as we receive the rest that comes from grace. Transformation is at hand.

Shame becomes grace, and brokenness becomes healing and wholeness.

We're going to look again at the list of expressions of shame and see how they become expressions of grace. Again, I want you to scale these experiences of grace. Rate both your family of origin and your current family unit. Think on a scale of 1 – 10 and write down how you would rate the presence of these encouraging and healthy dynamics.

Characteristics of Grace Based Relationships

1.   Empowerment
2.   Excellence
3.   Responsibility
4.   Authenticity
5.   Reliability
6.   Respect/Honor
7.   Abstinence/Moderation
8.   Appropriate Anger & Hurt

Let's look a little deeper at these eight expressions of grace.

Control becomes Empowerment

Systems of grace that flourish with empowerment create an environment where **power is given away**. In a system of control, one person in the relationship exerts their power over another. Control subdues and limits others in the system. In a system of empowerment, someone – or perhaps everyone – is intentionally and graciously giving their power away. Initially, that looks like someone using their power on behalf of another – not to rescue them, but to enable them to claim their own dignity, strength, and influence. I picture empowerment like somebody coming up underneath and lifting another up so that they can stand on their own. Empowerment means using my own power to engage, inspire, and encourage someone else's power.

Think about the family you grew up in. Maybe you had an empowering dad or mom, brother or sister. Maybe it was your aunt, or uncle, or grandpa, or grandma. And they were *powerful* in some way. Maybe they were courageous. Maybe they had a good heart. Maybe they were full of strength, and they went to bat for you. They helped you out. They had your back, and then they transferred that power to you. You became more free and more whole and more healthy because someone empowered you to be so.

Think about the dynamic of your current family unit. How much empowerment is going on both through you and for you? Where do you see power being given away?

Perfectionism becomes Excellence

Systems of grace characterized by excellence create an environment where **doing the very best you can is enough**. While perfectionism creates a never-ending ladder to climb, excellence allows for there to be a finish line. Excellence celebrates achievement and success, because excellence means giving something your very best. And yet, excellence says that there is an end to the giving and the doing, and that your best is always enough. Excellence allows for different people to be different because of personality and talent and skill. There is no one mark of perfection to hit; rather, there is whole a spectrum of becoming to applaud. Excellence allows for personalization to happen, and for an individual's unique gifts to shine and be commended. It also allows for the reality that not everyone is great at everything, so weakness is just as welcomed as strength.

My son is good at football, and my daughter is good at soccer. Both are excellent, and both are different! They excel in their own sport, but not in each other's. This is a healthy dynamic in a family, where excellence is celebrated and perfection is not required.

Back in the day, when I was younger, I was much better at playing football than I was at being a gymnast. Excellence allows for me to have a gift and a skill set, and to be able to do some things better than other things. Excellence is doing the best I can with what I bring to the table, and feeling good and settled about that. Excellence acknowledges that someone else brings other things to the table and that they might be way better at those things than I am. Excellence doesn't compare skills, excellence simply celebrates them.

So, think about the family you grew up in. Think about if there were places or people that allowed opportunity for excellence and affirmed whatever that was for you. Did you feel valued for the unique skills that you brought to the table? Did you feel celebrated in pursuing your individual path of growth?

Now think about your current family unit. Is there comparison going on in terms of achievement? Or is there a celebration of each person's unique strengths?

Blame becomes Responsibility

The next characteristic of grace-based relationships is taking appropriate responsibility, which means that **individuals step up to be accountable for their own thoughts, actions, intentions, and behaviors.** In systems of blame, the theory is that when something goes wrong, it's someone else's fault. In a system of responsibility, the shift is *not,* "now everything is my fault." The shift is, "I will take the responsibility for whatever ways I contributed to the problem." The blame does not shift to the self, because blame is released altogether. Instead, the dynamic involves integrity: each person owning the appropriate responsibility for their own contributions to any given situation.

In recovery circles, they talk about "keeping my own side of the street clean." I like that metaphor. The mess isn't usually about any one person. But if I choose the integrity to admit when my own side of the street is in disarray, and I choose the maturity to clean up that part of it, then I'm doing the work I need to do to keep myself in a good place with God and my other relationships. I'm not going to take responsibility for *your* side of the street, because that's not mine to do. That wouldn't be appropriate for me to wander over to your yard and start hauling away your mess. But it would also not be appropriate for me to start blaming you for a disaster of a street, when I have contributed to the mess in the first place.

Think about the family you grew up in. Were people encouraged to take appropriate responsibility for themselves? Did you see an example of taking ownership of mistakes and of making amends when it was right to do so? Think about your family unit now. What is the dynamic of blame versus taking appropriate responsibility?

Denial becomes Authenticity

Systems of grace characterized by authenticity create an environment where **everyone is accepted for who they really are and how they really feel**. Authenticity means being honest about the good, the bad, and the ugly. Families that lean into authenticity choose grace for exactly who God made each individual to be. Flaws and brokenness and problems are accepted, and sharing those things in an authentic way is celebrated. A shame-based system of denial insists that individuals cover their flaws and hide their feelings. In a system of authenticity, true feelings and emotions are important and validated.

Think about the system in your family of origin. Were you invited to share your true, authentic self and feelings? Did you feel accepted for who God made you to be? Did your family allow people to be authentic within the system? And think about your current family dynamic. How easy is it for the people in your family to express their genuine emotions and true selves?

Unreliability becomes Reliability

Alright, this one isn't particularly creative as far as the words go, but it's the best way of expressing the transformation. While systems based in shame can be characterized by unreliability, systems based in grace demonstrate reliability. Simply, a system of reliability means that **people are consistent and follow through on what they say they will do**. The grace of reliability builds trust in people and trust in the family system. There is a feeling of security and confidence that people in the system can depend on each other.

I must say that I had a very reliable family growing up. I could trust them to follow through and do what they said they would do or be where they said they would be. I could depend on them to have my back. Reliability builds trust, and it allows people in the system to have a sense of confidence and esteem in themselves. It creates a dynamic where people feel able to move forward and take risks, because they can count on their family system to be there for them no matter what.

Think about your family of origin. Did they follow through on things? Was there a dynamic of trust and interdependence? Think about your family now. Are the people closest to you able to count on you? Are you able to count on them?

Disqualification becomes Respect and Honor

Systems of grace characterized by respect and honor create an environment where **each individual is validated as a human being that deserves equal consideration**. While disqualification sends the message that anyone who tries to talk about the problem *is the problem*, respect and honor validate each person's perspectives. The grace of respect and honor says that each person is made in the image of God, and each person has a voice that is valued. Respect and honor do not evaluate behavior or appearance or accomplishment as a qualification for being allowed to have an opinion; respect and honor say that all opinions are valid and worth considering.

Think back about the way you grew up. Were people in your family of origin respected and honored as human beings deserving consideration? Did you feel like you could bring up problems without being accused of being the problem? Think about your current system. Are opinions and perspectives welcomed from all?

Addictions become Abstinence or Moderation

Grace based systems develop practices that **allow for appropriateness and balance in places that could be out of balance**. While the weight of shame can cause addictions in systems that do not provide practices for maintaining balance, the release of grace lifts that weight and provides a framework for healthy living. In some cases where the behavior can be damaging, like drugs or pornography, abstinence is necessary, so the system comes alongside individuals to encourage that. In other cases where the behavior needs to be kept in balance, like eating or exercising, a grace-based system provides an environment of healthy moderation. Choosing abstinence or moderation is the antithesis of shame, because it is allowing light to permeate the places where shame could otherwise keep us trapped in the dark.

Think about your family of origin. Did you see abstinence and/or moderation practiced and exampled? Was healthy balance celebrated and encouraged? Were there systems and practices in place that provided a framework for moderation? Then think about your current system. How would you rate the work of grace in providing a healthy balance for everyone in the family?

Rage becomes Appropriate Anger or Hurt

Grace based relationships build a system where **people are allowed to make healthy expressions of their pain**. We defined rage as out-of-control anger that comes from a shame-based system; grace-based systems have an understanding that appropriate anger and hurt are healthy and part of being human. Things are going to happen in life where we're going to be angry and hurt. Life is not always fair, and the injustice we experience will bring up righteous anger and legitimate hurt. Expressing those things in appropriate ways is part of a grace-based system. There is nothing shameful about healthy pain.

Think about your family of origin. Did you see healthy expressions of anger as part of your upbringing? Were you taught to express your hurt in ways where it could be spoken to and healed? How about now? What does the dynamic of anger do in your current system? Does it feel healthy and appropriate?

As you look at the scale and the ratings you have made in each of these categories, I hope it has brought you some encouragement. Perhaps you were able to find a place of grace in your family of origin, even just one area where you can build on. My encouragement to you is to start with any strength that you can find, and then ask God to build on that as you move forward.

As you think about your current relationships with significant people in your life right now, I bet you'll be able to identify some places of strength that now show up in your current relationships. If you grew up in a system where authenticity was valued, for example, you probably see authenticity in your current relationships. And if you don't, that's great place to start to use something that was a strength from the past! That might be the perfect place for you to practice a grace-based approach to your current relationships with other people today.

A Prayer

Even if you didn't find much grace in the family you grew up in, God will still come alongside you and begin to bring grace into the relationships you have today. Maybe He will use a friend, a neighbor, a priest, or professional counselor. God reaches out to us through people. That is where we experience His grace. His strength is always a place to start. God is welcoming you to live freely and lightly, in the unforced rhythms of grace. This truth is both a challenge and an invitation, but the result of his grace is freedom and healing and rest for your soul. As we close this chapter, allow me to pray those things over you.

Wonderful Counselor, we do thank you for the places of strength and places of grace that we can see in our past and in our present. We see those things as affirmation, as hope that we have a place to build on and move forward from. Ultimately, we get from you, even if we didn't get much of it from the families that we grew up in. Help every one of us to practice your grace and rest, and to look for opportunities to engage our relationships from a place of grace. Keep us conscious of how we treat others, and keep us conscious of your grace for us. We love you. We're overwhelmed by your love for us. In Jesus name, Amen.

CHAPTER SIX

Forgiveness

As we progress in our journey of trading shame for grace, we come to the question of forgiveness.

Can we forgive?

Forgiveness is an essential element to our healing and transformation. Without it, those places of pain in our past can never be truly healed. We must offer forgiveness to others, and we must offer forgiveness to ourselves. In our journey so far, we've been able to deal with some of the places of shame in our past and in our present by acknowledging them and receiving grace into them. As we work to replace pieces of our shame with the reality of grace, the process becomes more and more difficult. We discover the places where forgiveness is necessary, and we are faced with the reality that forgiveness is *hard*. Asking for forgiveness is hard. Receiving forgiveness is hard. Offering forgiveness is hard. Uncovering the hurts that require forgiveness is hard. And yet, it is a vital practice for our healing.

So, let's venture into a conversation about forgiveness and second chances. Let's allow space for the reality that it will be a journey. Let's remember that there's a process that happens as we deal with acceptance and forgiveness, both for ourselves and for others.

Spiritual Foundation: The World Is Not A Stage

In order to take the first steps towards understanding and embracing forgiveness, let's look at the words of Jesus from Matthew 6:1-15 in the Message.

> *"Be especially careful when you are trying to be good so that you don't make a performance out of it. It might be good theater, but the God who made you won't be applauding.*
>
> *When you do something for someone else, don't call attention to yourself. You've seen them in action, I'm sure—'play-actors' I call them—treating prayer meeting and street corner alike as a stage, acting compassionate as long as someone is watching, playing to the crowds. They get applause, true, but that's all they get. When you help someone out, don't think about how it looks. Just do it—quietly and unobtrusively. That is the way your God, who*

conceived you in love, working behind the scenes, helps you out.

And when you come before God, don't turn that into a theatrical production either. All these people making a regular show out of their prayers, hoping for stardom! Do you think God sits in a box seat?

Here's what I want you to do: Find a quiet, secluded place so you won't be tempted to role-play before God. Just be there as simply and honestly as you can manage. The focus will shift from you to God, and you will begin to sense his grace.

The world is full of so-called prayer warriors who are prayer-ignorant. They're full of formulas and programs and advice, peddling techniques for getting what you want from God. Don't fall for that nonsense. This is your Father you are dealing with, and he knows better than you what you need. With a God like this loving you, you can pray very simply. Like this:

Our Father in heaven,
Reveal who you are.
Set the world right;

Do what's best—

as above, so below.

Keep us alive with three square meals.

Keep us forgiven with you and forgiving others.

Keep us safe from ourselves and the Devil.

You're in charge!

You can do anything you want!

You're ablaze in beauty!

Yes. Yes. Yes.

In prayer there is a connection between what God does and what you do. You can't get forgiveness from God, for instance, without also forgiving others. If you refuse to do your part, you cut yourself off from God's part."

Matthew 6:1-15 MSG

These words of Jesus probably don't help you feel like the process of forgiveness will be any easier than you first suspected, do they? It will not be easy, because it cannot be forced or fake. For forgiveness to have any healing power, it has to be genuine.

Forgiveness is not a staged production or a rallied effort; it is an authentic overflow of God's Spirit in and to us.

Forgiveness cannot be fully mustered from our moral muscle; it must be made complete by the grace of the Father that flows through us. And yet, in order for His grace to flow, we must be willing. We must shift our focus from ourselves to God, so that we can begin to sense His grace. We must receive His forgiveness for our own wrongdoings, so that we can in turn offer it to those who have wronged us.

This, dear friends, is the path to healing.

The Process of Forgiveness

Take a few moments to let this definition of forgiveness absorb into your soul:

> *Forgiveness is understanding and holding the pain of another; it is compassion. Forgiveness is the acceptance of our own brokenness, yours and mine. Forgiveness is letting go of unrealistic expectations of others and of the desire that they be other than they are. Forgiveness is liberating others to be themselves, not making them feel guilty for what may have been ... Forgiveness is peacemaking struggling to create unity, to build one*

body, to heal the broken body of humanity.[31]

I don't know about you, but when I read those words, I feel the Spirit alive in them. And I pray that this sort of forgiveness will flourish in me and around me. I pray the same for you.

Here's something we have to remember as we engage this conversation:

Forgiveness is a process. It's not an event.

It takes time!

Forgiveness takes time, and it's relational. It's about both the giving and receiving. It's about all sorts of internal work around the pain. And it's about allowing the Spirit of God to breathe grace into every heart involved.

Experts say that there is a four-step process that we must go through to receive forgiveness: confession, contrition, conversion, and atonement.[32]

---

[31] Varnier, Jean. *The Broken Body: Journey to Wholeness*. Darton Longman & Todd Ltd, 1988, Reprinted 2018, p. 106.

[32] Hampton, Rick. "Can You Forgive? America's About Second Chances, Will Lance Get His?", *USA Today*, 18 Jan 2013.

Confession involves admitting that you did it, and that you understand that it's wrong. *Contrition* means actually being sorry that you did it, acknowledging that it hurt people. *Conversion* means taking action that shows you learned from it and that you will work to not do it again. *Atonement* is positive action taken to make amends for the negative action.

Confession, being contrite, going through a conversion process, and ultimately making atonement are the four steps to receiving forgiveness. I love that, but I want to challenge us to take it a couple layers deeper as we engage the process and acknowledge the time it takes.

First of all, let's think about the idea of "forgetting". We have all heard the phrase, "forgive and forget". But should that really be the goal? Is it even possible? I don't think so. We don't always forget the wounds that have been inflicted on us. We may not forget the wounds that we've caused other people. *I think the power in forgiveness is in forgiving and remembering, not forgetting*. Let's be honest. Let's be *authentic* with the fact that those things may never go away. They will lessen over time, but if I choose to forgive or receive forgiveness, it may mean that I need to manage some thoughts or memories or feelings as I heal. I may never fully forget those places of hurt and betrayal and harm.

The second challenge I have is for us to choose to be a people of second chances. Isn't that who Jesus was? Most definitely, and I believe we are called to be the same. I challenge us to give the grace of second chances, but not just because somebody "earned it" by going through this four-step process of receiving forgiveness. ***The grace of second chances is about allowing people to go through a process of healing and growth and change.*** It's about affirming and celebrating their journey with the full knowledge that we may find ourselves on the end of needing to have that second chance given to us.

Now, let me try to be clear. I'm not suggesting that you should get taken advantage of over and over and over again. You may need to put some limits and boundaries in place. You may need to say no, but your heart can stay in a place of offering forgiveness even as a person is going through the process of their own healing.

The same is true when we are on the receiving end. You may need to ask somebody for forgiveness again and again and again, as you're in the process of working through your own path of growth and healing. You may need to accept the boundaries someone else has to put in place during that journey, but you can also receive the grace of second chances. I hope and pray that we will become a people, a family, a place, a church of second chances and of wisdom as we practice what it means to forgive, to remember, and to find places of growth and healing.

Forgiveness and Shame

So what about forgiveness as it specifically relates to our shame? Smedes put together a five-step process of forgiveness about shame, and I believe it offers a simple but comprehensive approach.

1. Figure out whose shame it really is.

2. Surrender the right to get even.

3. Allow a transformation to begin in your heart, where you see the shamer through different eyes.

4. Allow for an unfreezing of your hard heart.

5. Over much time, acceptance is offered to the one who shamed you (with boundaries).[33]

Let's unpack that a bit.

Figure out whose shame it really is. There are times in life for all of us when someone speaks shame over us, but we have actually done nothing to deserve that shame. Frequently, we take the shame on, but it isn't actually ours. It isn't about us. We are just the victim of someone else's pain as they sort through their own struggles. It is imperative that we learn to make the distinction about what shame is about our own

---

[33] Smedes, Lewis. ***Shame and Grace.*** New York, Zondervan Publishing, 1993, pp. 134-136.

brokenness and what shame is about someone else's.

Surrender the right to get even. Remember when I told you earlier that *life isn't fair, but life is good?* This is one of those places. It may not seem fair to surrender our right to get even, but it is good. By the way, getting even is an illusion. We're talking about emotional and relational connectedness. You can never be "even". I have to give up the right to get even, and I have to realize that the interpersonal struggle may never be completely resolved. I may have to make sense of some hurt in my own life without feeling complete resolution. I may have to learn how to let go and move forward. That's part of the process of forgiveness. Surrender.

Allow a transformation to begin in your heart, where you see the shamer through different eyes. For transformation to occur, we have to come to the place where we develop empathy and understanding. This means that we see the broader context. We see the bigger picture. We understand that people who shame people were once shamed themselves. An understanding develops that the brokenness didn't start with us, with our contribution to the cycle. We see that there has been a generational cycle that's been going on, one that goes all the way back to Adam and Eve, one that has been passed down through families of origin on all sides. As we start to see and understand people who have hurt us in a broader context, it makes more sense to see that they were doing the best that they could. We begin to believe they were doing what they knew to do, and empathy emerges. We begin to allow the space and time they need for their own growth and healing.

Allow for an unfreezing of your hard heart. This language may sound extreme. You may not feel that your heart is frozen or hard. But the reality is that those sorts of defense mechanisms are the human response to the hurt caused by layers of unfair shame. It is not wrong for your heart to be hard. It is human. When the time for healing comes, you will know how to allow the spirit of God to soften your heart again. That is the work of grace. The process of forgiveness brings us to a place of becoming more tender, more gentle, and more understanding of what was really going on for the people who have shamed us. As that happens, our hardened hearts will soften.

Over much time, acceptance is offered to the one who shamed you. This is a process that takes time, and it is once again important to reiterate the need for boundaries. This does not mean that you just open yourself up to be taken advantage of and mistreated. This does not mean you accept more shame and have to go through the whole process over and over and over again with the same person or people. You may have to take some action in order to stop those things from happening. You may have to put some boundaries or limits in those relationships. That all goes with the territory in the process of forgiveness. Still, with healthy boundaries and limits in place, you can accept those who shame you as Beloved children of God. You can forgive and remember. You can practice the grace of the second chance.

I can tell you that I have lived this out. I've seen this happen firsthand in my own situations and in my own family. You might notice that I have purposely not told many personal stories about my own family of origin as we've journeyed through this material together. I could have shared those things, because I do have some places that have been challenges for me as I've matured over the years, as we all do. But I'll tell you what happened for me: as I made some sense of some of those things in my own life, God gave me kids, and thereby also gave me my own opportunities to screw up with them. I'll tell you, that's about the most humbling thing ever. And so instead of just pointing backwards at what people have done to me and where *they* screwed up along the way, I've been able to see my own mistakes and opportunities to choose something different. That perspective, while humbling and sometimes downright painful, has helped me with this process of forgiveness.

When I've looked backwards in an attempt to be honest and authentic with some hurts and challenges from my past, I've seen my own mistakes, too. I have had to go to my kids and ask for forgiveness, and to work things out in my own family. That's what happens when we step back and see the broader picture, when we become aware of relationships moving from generation to generation. The journey of forgiveness by the grace of God heals past, present, and future all at once.

Forgiveness and Building Shame Resilience

Brené Brown uses the term "shame resilience" as a way of describing the strength that comes by healing in our places of shame. Shame resilience *is the ability to recognize shame when we experience it, and move through it in a constructive way that allows us to maintain our authenticity and grow from our experience.*[34] believe that forgiveness is one of the most powerful effective ways to build our shame resilience.

I recall many victories with clients over the years as they learned to build shame resilience. Not too long ago, I was working with a young woman in ministry. Her name was Judy. She was processing through her own shame, from both her family of origin and her church. Her family had a real challenge with healthy boundaries, believing that they were

---

[34] Brown, Brené. *I Thought It Was Just Me (but it isn't): Making the Journey from "What Will People Think?" to "I Am Enough".* New York, Gotham, 2007. Kindle edition.

always supposed to put themselves last and sacrifice everything for others. This happened at the detriment of the family, many times. As she grew up and went into ministry, she found herself doing the same things. But gradually, over time, she started learning to say that little word that is so very hard for some of us ...*NO*. She learned to say it with her family, and then with people who always needed things from her. Eventually she learned to say it to people at her church and other places in her life.

She was nervous and afraid as she learned to put up boundaries, but do you know what? She survived! The people around her survived, and some of them even decided that they needed to take care of themselves, too. And much like the tough skin that builds up on your fingers from playing and practicing a guitar over and over, she got stronger, and it became easier to say no. After a while, her "yes" became a real yes, and her "no" became a real no. She learned to celebrate the "no" as much as the "yes"! That is building up shame resiliency.

Part of the goal with the whole process of healing and forgiveness is to build resiliency to when we go through an experience that would previously have produced shame. We can actually develop the mental and spiritual muscle to be able to process experiences differently and therefore diminish the amount of shame that is produced as a result of those experiences.

Brown lists four characteristics of shame resilience:

1. The ability to recognize and understand shame triggers
2. High levels of awareness about my shame web
3. The willingness to reach out to others
4. The ability to speak about my shame[35]

Let's break those down and we will see how the process of forgiveness leads us to shame resilience

Shame triggers are the things that send us nearly instantly to a place of shame. If we are going to build shame resilience, we have to become aware of those things so that we can proactively respond when a shame trigger experience happens. For example, before we experience healing of our shame, we are susceptible to messages that tell us who we are supposed to be and how we are supposed to act. If we fail to be or do those things, we experience shame. But as we go through the process of forgiveness, we begin to see where those messages have come from. We begin to understand why they have existed, and we begin to see the truth about who we really are. Not only that, but as we offer forgiveness to those who have perpetuated those shame triggers, we also take

---

[35] Brown, Brené. *I Thought It Was Just Me (but it isn't): Making the Journey from "What Will People Think?" to "I Am Enough"*. New York, Gotham, 2007. Kindle edition.

away their power to continue to shame us. Those messages are highlighted for what they are: lies. As our hearts soften and our empathy grows through the work of forgiveness, we are able to identify the triggers and not fall prey to their accusations.

Often for men, shame triggers are around respect. For women, shame triggers are around love and affirmation.[36] When I feel disrespected, it pushes the shame trigger in me. I'm aware of that, and I know I have to watch that place for me. I have to remember the work I have done around it and the forgiveness I have already offered those who have disrespected me in the past. When I lean into the reality of that journey, I lean out of the way of the shame.

High levels of awareness about the shame web are also essential to shame resilience. Not only do we need to be aware of the triggers, we need to be aware about our environment, our community. There may be people or situations that will consistently bring up your shame triggers. Your highest levels of awareness about those situations and people will come in the wake of your journey towards forgiveness. As you participate in the work of forgiveness, your awareness grows. Your boundaries become more secure, and your filters

[36] Brown, Brené. *I Thought It Was Just Me (but it isn't): Making the Journey from "What Will People Think?" to "I Am Enough"*.New York, Gotham, 2007. Kindle edition.

become more stable. These things are vital for long term shame resilience.

A willingness to reach out to others for honest and healing conversations is a key characteristic of shame resilience. Not only do you need to have a safety net of people that you can turn to for truth and grace when you feel a wave of shame coming on, you also need to be able to be honest with those who are causing the feelings of shame. If you have entered into a journey for forgiveness towards those people, it is far easier to have the honest conversations necessary to healthily process the experience of shame. When you have already accepted them as they are and forgiven them, you can stand up for the truth about yourself with boldness and compassion.

The ability to speak about our shame builds shame resilience. Shame thrives in the dark. Shame thrives in silence. We break the power of shame and we build shame resilience as we connect with others and as we speak openly and honestly about those places of hurt and shame. Forgiveness is the bridge that allows us to build those connections and to be honest and vulnerable about our places of shame. As we open our hearts to the healing work of forgiveness, we grasp the importance of bringing things into the light.

Your Journey of Forgiveness

It is likely that as you have read this chapter, you have felt the need to give or receive forgiveness. This is good. The journey of forgiveness is one that we will always be on because, as humans, we will all continue to need it. I encourage you to take a few moments to think about your current relationships. You may realize that you are in a space where you need to have a conversation with someone, or take some time for reflection on your own. You may need to offer someone forgiveness for something you have been holding onto. You may need to finally let it go. You may need to ask forgiveness for your own contributions to someone else's shame. Invite God into those places today, and reflect on the next steps you can take on your journey of forgiveness.

Secondly, I would invite you to consider where and how are you going to build some shame resiliency in your life. Where are you in the process of becoming healthier and setting some limits or boundaries? Where can you make a courageous choice to bring something into the light and to speak vulnerably about it? And how can forgiveness lead you down the path of resilience? Imagine that journey of healing in your own story.

I'll never forget one time of going to my daughter to ask for forgiveness. She was about 5 years old at the time, and I had done some bonehead thing as a parent. I don't remember all the details of what I did, because there were plenty of opportunities for this to have happened. I had probably scolded her too hard, or raised my voice too loud, or done something that kind of scared her and made her cry. I felt pretty bad.

I remember going into her bedroom and kneeling down by the bed next to her and saying, "Honey, I'm sorry. Dad lost his temper. Dad raised his voice. He didn't do a very good job there. Will you forgive me for that?"

And she simply put her hand on my shoulder and looked deep into my eyes and said, "It's okay, Daddy. I forgive you."

That moment of forgiveness floored me. It was so humbling. It was so healing. I had acknowledged my shame and she had met it with grace. And light washed over the both of us in that moment. I was forgiven.

It is difficult to see the places where I need to grow and change and shift. And it is even more difficult to realize that the places that were the most challenging around shame for me growing up have become the very same places that I have to work on the hardest as an adult. It is so easy to fall into the patterns of behavior of our family of origin, to perpetuate a cycle that continues to bring shame.

The cycle can be stopped.

Grace and forgiveness are the path to change and freedom.

A Prayer

Father God, I want to thank you that you are in the business of forgiving. Every one of us is in need of that forgiveness. As we continue to look at shame in our lives, we see there's a connection between the forgiveness that we work out with you and the forgiveness that we work out in all of our key relationships with each other. Thank you that you were willing to go above and beyond to do anything necessary, to send your son for our ultimate forgiveness. Help us to practice giving and receiving forgiveness. Help us to find our way in moving forward with health and vulnerability and courage in our relationships. We need your strength and power to do that. We know that we can't do it on our own. We love you. Thank you for your love for us. In Jesus name, Amen.

CHAPTER SEVEN

A Life of Grace

We have gone on quite a journey together, exploring our shame and opening our minds and hearts to the healing power of grace and forgiveness. And yet, this is only the beginning. There is so much more to a life of grace, and we all have much to learn and discover and experience as we allow the work of God to heal us and make us whole.

Spiritual Foundation: Living by the Spirit's Power

There is a whole lot of work around shame and grace that we can do on our own. It's good, important work and I'm proud of us for doing it! However, as we have already discovered, there's something about the power of the Holy Spirit that can do work in us that we can't do ourselves. Truly, a life of grace involves living by the Spirit's power.

Eugene Peterson's beautiful interpretation of Paul's words about this is found in Galatians 5:22 – 6:5 MSG.

> *"But what happens when we live God's way? He brings*

gifts into our lives, much the same way that fruit appears in an orchard—things like affection for others, exuberance about life, serenity. We develop a willingness to stick with things, a sense of compassion in the heart, and a conviction that a basic holiness permeates things and people. We find ourselves involved in loyal commitments, not needing to force our way in life, able to marshal and direct our energies wisely.

Legalism is helpless in bringing this about; it only gets in the way. Among those who belong to Christ, everything connected with getting our own way and mindlessly responding to what everyone else calls necessities is killed off for good—crucified.

Since this is the kind of life we have chosen, the life of the Spirit, let us make sure that we do not just hold it as an idea in our heads or a sentiment in our hearts, but work out its implications in every detail of our lives. That means we will not compare ourselves with each other as if one of us were better and another worse. We have far more interesting things to do with our lives. Each of us is an original.

*Live creatively, friends. If someone falls into sin,
forgivingly restore him, saving your critical comments
for yourself. You might be needing forgiveness before the
day's out. Stoop down and reach out to those who are
oppressed. Share their burdens, and so complete
Christ's law. If you think you are too good for that, you
are badly deceived.*

*Make a careful exploration of who you are and the
work you have been given, and then sink yourself into
that. Don't be impressed with yourself. Don't compare
yourself with others. Each of you must take
responsibility for doing the creative best you can with
your own life."*

Galatians 5:22 – 6:5 MSG

What a powerful passage! I think we could read this every single day, out loud, and it wouldn't be too much. This is a life of grace.

One of the pieces that feels most important to me in this text is that as we do this work around shame and live this life of grace, it should *permeate every aspect of our lives*. This isn't about behaving one way on Sunday mornings and a completely different way the rest of the week. This isn't about working towards healing in one relationship while actively damaging another. ***This is about commitment to being a person of integrity.*** Integrity means that we choose to be honest and authentic with our good and our bad, our strengths and our flaws. This is about showing up the same way on Sunday as you do on Monday, and Tuesday, and Wednesday, and throughout the week. This is about being a person who pursues health in your marriage as well as your work relationships. This is about being a person who is living by the power of the Spirit and allowing the Spirit access to every area of your life.

The second piece that stands out to me in this passage is that the God of the universe says *you are an original*. We've heard this sort of talk before. "They broke the mold after you were made." "God made you special." And while it may sound trite, what we sometimes forget is that it is true! He made you who you are, and ***you have unique abilities and skills to make a difference in this world that nobody else can.*** Because of our originality, it is so important that we do not compare ourselves to others. Every time we do that, we come up short. You will always lose when you play the comparison game. The devastation that social media is causing our society is hugely impacted by our propensity for comparison. But a life animated by the Spirit has no need for such things.

The final piece of this exhortation from Paul here that I love is this picture of *making a careful exploration of who we are and what we've been given to do*. Doesn't that sound infinitely more fun and filling than a disappointing life of comparison? This careful exploration allows the Spirit to lead us on a discovery path inward, finding out just what we were created for and then leaning into it with the energy and blessing of God himself. And ***part of this work of careful exploration is our healing.***

The Healing of Shame

A life in Christ allows the Spirit to guide the healing process, which is a journey of recovery, release, repair, and reconnection.

As we ***recover*** shame scenes from the past, we begin to be honest with those places of brokenness. We relive those scenes. We remember them. We talk about them. We engage with them. We're honest with them. As we cope with our shame, we must again walk through those events and experiences. The work of the Spirit is evident here as it calls these experiences to mind and empowers us with courage to face them.

As we do that, we ***release*** some of the feelings and layers that are embedded in those memories. We make them conscious, and then we take charge over them. In that process we're reshaping and reframing the old scenes by creating new scenes and new memories and new connections and new relationships. The work of the Spirit is evident here in that the reframing comes most powerfully from seeing our experiences through the lens of God's grace.

The next step in the journey is to **repair** some of the damage that has been done. This reparation can be accomplished in many ways, but it always starts with a reclamation of our own power. When we realize that others do not truly hold the power to speak shame over us, then we can begin to speak grace and blessing in its place. The work of the Spirit takes it a step farther, speaking the truth of our identity as Beloved sons and daughters of God Himself. The Spirit brings grace and blessing in the place of shame that is powerful enough to free us from it forever.

Finally, we **reconnect**. We seek support, acceptance, and empathy. We reconnect our hearts with other people, either in new, trusted relationships or newly healed relationships from our past. We utilize playful and lighthearted humor to normalize our human experience and some of the challenges that we've had along the way. The Spirit draws us to reconnect not only with our families and friends and colleagues, but with God, so that we may live every day in the truth of his grace.

Sadly, in nearly 30 years as a professional counselor and

minister, I have worked with many couples where affairs have ripped relationships apart. An affair is one of the very deepest betrayals of trust and love. It is incredibly destructive. And if I had not seen what I'm about to tell you next firsthand, I probably wouldn't believe it. I have permission to tell this story, but I will only share an overview to protect the couple.

A middle-aged man – let's call him Fred – came to see me for help in dealing with an affair he was in. His wife, Janet, did not know about it. But this wasn't just any affair; he was living two lives. While he was legally married and had a family here on the west coast, he also had another woman and family on the east coast. He wanted to come clean before his wife and God. I will never forget the session where he told his wife of the ongoing affair. She wept so hard. She was, rightly, so angry. His behaviors were so inappropriate, damaging, and overwhelming. It would have been no surprise to me if their marriage could just not survive this.

Over time, we helped him end all the unhealthy relationships, seek forgiveness, make amends, and change his addictive ways. He entered into an ongoing process of change and forgiveness with his wife and with God. After over a year of hard work, he and his wife were still together. I remember receiving a phone call from them on their "new" 5-year anniversary, and their marriage was as healthy as it had ever been. This outcome was a testament first to a God of restoration and grace. Second, to the wife who refused to lose her marriage, who chose forgiveness and grace by the strength of Christ within her. And lastly, to the man who *did the work* to change his behaviors.

Fred *recovered* the shame in his past, walking through the reality of the whole situation with his counselor, his wife, and his trusted friends. He *released* the shame that was holding him captive so that he could do the work of *repairing* the damage he had done. He *reconnected* with his wife and with God, accepting forgiveness.

Let me be clear. It doesn't always work out this way! In fact, sadly, I have worked with many other couples that could not make it through the devastating effects of an affair. But it is possible. Grace makes healing possible. Whether the healing comes in a reconciliation of a restored relationship or in the closure of a broken one, grace leads to healing.

The Brain-Shame Healing Connection

There is some astounding research that continues to be developed around the connection between the brain and shame, and the healing connection that happens there. Interpersonal neurobiology is the latest and greatest in my field, and we still have so much to discover. The more the counseling profession continues to learn, the more we realize that our brains are truly an amazing creation.

What we have discovered is that some of the experiences of brokenness and shame in our childhoods have literally burned physical grooves between points in our brains that carry forward into adulthood. The more times we've had similar shaming experiences, the deeper the grooves were cut in our brains. When we get to adulthood, our reactions to shame triggers are ingrained and almost involuntary. We don't even have to think when we start to feel shame coming on, because our brain responds instantly.

Michael Lewis expounds on this research in his book, *Shame: The Exposed Self.* "Shame makes its way into our stories at an early age. So early, in fact that we usually have no conscious memory of our initial encounters with it. This can take place as early as 15-18 months, and usually involves a child's response to someone's nonverbal cues-that interrupt whatever the child may be doing, delivering a subtle but underlying felt message of disapproval."[37]

The great news about this is that our brains can change and heal. It takes effort and work to retrain your brain, but you can do it. Every time you make a choice to do something

---

[37] Lewis, Michael. *Shame: The Exposed Self.* New York, Simon and Schuster, 1992, pp 91- 96.

healthy and respond in a different way to shame, you change the pathway in your brain.It[38] is truly incredible what science is teaching us. When I began in this field of study, we sort of thought these things were true, and had a lot of theories about it. But now we have the ability with imaging to see what's actually happening in the brain.

Your right brain is your creative side. It's where your feelings are. It's where your senses are. It's where you pick up on facial expressions, tone of voice, and other non-verbal social and emotional cues. It develops *before* language begins to form in your brain. Our first couple of years of life, it's like our antennae are up and we are picking up on all kinds of emotional interactions between people. We sense all the cues and begin to learn them, but we don't have words for them yet.

Your left brain adds language and logic and linear thinking and processing. This is where you begin to put words to your experiences and feelings. You begin to have a way to articulate all those right brain impressions you've had for two years. The brain's ability to create new neurons, make new connections, and prune old, negative connections is called

[38] Thompson, Curt. *Anatomy of the Soul: Surprising Connections between Neuroscience and Spiritual Practices That Can Transform Your Life and Relationships*. Carrollton, TX, Tyndale, 2010, p. 47.

neuroplasticity.[39] Curt Thompson explains it like this:

> *Neurons that fire together wire together. Evidence accumulated over the last three decades indicates that brain cells have greater capacity for adaptation and regeneration than was previously believed. This characteristic is generally referred to as neuroplasticity. This property of neurons allows for the connection between different domains of the brain, and thereby different functional components such as sensations, images, feelings, thoughts and bodily actions.*[40]

This dynamic development of our brains gives us incredible hope. We can change. We can physically rewrite neural pathways and heal broken patterns. We were created with the ability to choose new end games for the pain and brokenness we experience. We can teach ourselves to instantly respond to shame triggers with the attributes of grace instead of the attributes of shame. Instead of control, we can learn empowerment. Instead of perfectionism, we can learn excellence. Instead of blame, we can learn responsibility. And

---

[39] Thompson, Curt. *The Soul of Shame.* Downers Grove, IL, InterVarsity Press, 2015, p. 48.

[40] Thompson, Curt. *The Soul of Shame.* Downers Grove, IL, InterVarsity Press, 2015, p. 47.

on the list goes.

The best part is, we can do better than *learn* these things.

> ***We can develop neural pathways so that our brain responds intuitively with these healthy behaviors of grace.***

Here's how Thompson puts it: "The brain is constantly scanning the internal and external landscape, comparing the present to the past in order to prepare the body for the future."[41]

Let me say that again. Your brain is constantly scanning the world – your relationships, emotions, circumstances, experiences – and comparing what's happening right now to things that have happened in the past. This assessment helps your brain to prepare you for the future.

This is why your work around shame is so hugely important. As you mend emotional and relational brokenness, you are preparing your brain to react differently in the future! As you reflect on your painful narratives and your family of origin, and as you find understanding and forgiveness, the process rewires your brain. The story in the past becomes a different

---

[41] Thompson, Curt. *Anatomy of the Soul: Surprising Connections between Neuroscience and Spiritual Practices That Can Transform Your Life and Relationships.* Carrollton, TX, Tyndale, 2010, p. 185.

story because of the work you are doing in the present, and your responses in the future will be different because of the work you are doing in the present. Amazing!

Do you remember your second birthday party? Who was there? Where was it? Can you remember what kind of cake you had at your third birthday party, or if there was a clown, or balloons? If you do, the reason you remember it is not because you actually remember it. You "remember" it because you have heard stories about it. You've seen pictures or video, or grandma has told you some special details. You may have been a six or seven-year-old kid when you looked at some pictures of your third birthday party, and because of that, you feel like you remember it. When we retell our stories, our brain takes it in as if experiencing it for the first time.

As a counselor, this is a powerful tool for healing. People come into my office and tell me their stories. They tell me their hurt, they tell me their shame, they tell me their problems. And often, I don't have answers. I don't have the advice they need to fix those things or make them go away. But do you know what I always have? I have the very same things you always have: the ability to listen and the ability to offer empathy. That can sometimes be all that anyone needs to find their own path towards health.

Remember all the way back to our silly toilet paper pyramid

story at the beginning of this book? The number one thing they found in the people who watched the embarrassing act of knocking over the toilet paper was *care and empathy*. I'm telling you, that matters. When people tell you their stories, you can listen, you can care, you can offer them empathy. You are reshaping the story and the hurt.

And empathy is so healing. When we give and receive empathy, we are most like God. Walking in the steps of another, the best we can, forces us to put our own thoughts, biases, and opinions on hold, at least for a moment, while we deeply connect with another. When you say, "that makes sense to me", you are practicing deep connection with another. When you validate someone, which can be done without agreeing with them, by the way, you connect deeply with another.

When people do that for you, they're reshaping the story that you remember. How healing is that? I can never go back and make what happened in the past not happen, but I can come alongside another and offer care and listening and empathy that will actually change their perceived experience and rewire their brain.

I hope you can see the possibility in these discoveries. I hope that you will lean into the pursuit of telling and listening to stories with care and empathy and forgiveness and compassion. As we tell our stories and feel witnessed and validated, we heal. As we heal, our stories are reshaped into positive experiences of grace.

Capture the Moment

Let's think a little more into some tangible action steps in your process of healing from shame. One of the most important things you can do is to capture the moment: notice the feelings, thoughts, and experiences in the moment of shame. A colleague of mine at George Fox University writes about this idea of "capturing the moment" in an incredible article called, "When Perfect Fear Casts Out All Love."Sometimes[42] we have an exchange with someone that feels painful, and then we walk away and we're not really sure what just happened. We don't feel good about the experience, but if we aren't aware, we might not be able to put words to our feelings. We might wonder why we seem to be spiraling in the wake of what they said or did. We might invalidate our own pangs of pain and move on without much conscious thought, allowing a shame experience to add to our overall shame narrative.

In these times, we need to slow down and ask ourselves what

_____

[42] Thurston, Nancy. "When Perfect Fear Casts Out All Love." *Journal of Psychology and Christianity*, 13, 1994, pp. 69 – 75.

happened. What did the person say? What did I say in response? What is the pain that I am feeling about the exchange? Why do I really feel this pain? Is this pain related to shame? This is *breaking through that place of denial*. This is being honest with what's happening authentically in the moment in the relationship, and letting myself see it, hear it, feel it, and be present in the moment.

Once we have captured the moment and noticed the shame, it's important to put words to it. We can say to ourselves or to someone we trust, "You know what just happened? I'm feeling shame right now. I'm feeling invalidated. I'm feeling inferior. I'm feeling ridiculed. The pain I'm feeling is shame."

When we feel that sense in our gut that we will never be good enough, that's a moment of shame. When our eyes are pulled to the floor so that we can't even look at the other person's face, that's a moment of shame. When we feel judged and begin to second guess ourselves, that's a moment of shame.

Many people have never practiced an awareness of what these moments actually are. This awareness is hugely important to our healing. I encourage you to think about this the next time you encounter someone who tends to make you feel uncomfortable. Capture the moment of shame in the conversation. The awareness can change everything.

Coping Mechanisms

Every one of us has been impacted by shame – maybe a little, maybe a lot, maybe somewhere in the middle. And every one of us, when we have been impacted by shame, have learned how to try and cope with those circumstances. Coping mechanisms sort of have a negative connotation, but the truth is that God gave us coping mechanisms. He gave us the ability to deal with difficult things so that we could handle them and move on. We need coping mechanisms like perfecting, drinking, denying, intellectualizing, and inappropriate humor to help us manage our pain, to make sense of things in the moment, and to survive. Coping mechanisms serve a purpose in the moment, and sometimes we have to rely on coping mechanisms to get us through hard things, especially when it comes to a shame trigger.

The problem is, there are consequences that come with our coping mechanisms. And many of those get in the way of healthy behaviors and relationships. They might not serve us anymore, and they might block our path to growth and healing. And yet, because of the way our brains are wired and our hearts have built up defenses, we still keep these coping mechanisms in place and utilize them in unhealthy ways.

For example, if I was raised in a family that was full of really dysfunctional shame, one of my coping mechanisms might be that I literally imagine myself in an army tank. I feel like my family is at war, and part of the fire is directed at me. So in order to avoid feeling like I'm never good enough and there's something wrong with me, I just put that tank in between myself and the line of fire. Eventually, I learn to not even pay attention to the bullets flying around me, because I'm safe in my tank and I can survive it just fine.

Here's the problem: once the war is over, I can't just hop out of my tank. I get to adulthood, and maybe I'm not living with my family anymore. I don't need the defenses of my tank. I'm 18, then I'm 21, then I'm 25, then I'm married, then I have kids. And I'm still living life as if I'm in a tank, emotionally and relationally. I can't get close to people. I keep them at a distance. I can hardly see them. I try to drive a tank down Main Street, but it won't even fit on the road. It keeps ripping down signs and wires, and I'm making a mess everywhere I go.

Are you with me? Army tanks are not great places to parent from, be intimate from, or connect deeply with others from. But they are safe places. They serve a purpose.

And then what happens? Some well-meaning person, sometimes a pastor or a counselor, comes along and sees me in the tank and says, "Let's rip that tank off of you. Don't you see, you're causing all kinds of problems? You're driving a tank where there's no space for a tank. Get rid of that thing! All you need is a bicycle!"

And what do I do? I freak out. I'm not ready to be on a bicycle! There's a reason why I'm in a tank. The tank served a purpose for me and I can't just throw it away because someone tells me I don't need it anymore. How could I know that? What if I come out of it to find a war I can't survive out there?

This is where I need caring, loving people to come alongside me and say, "You know, that tank served a purpose for you. It got you to adulthood. You coped, and you made it. Thank God for that ability! But now it's time to downsize, okay? Let's not go from a tank to a bike, but let's put you in a Hummer! At least the Hummer will fit on the road, and there's windows in it. You can see out and in. You can be relational and connect with other people. And it even has lights and turn signals, so you can communicate! Let's help you be a little more vulnerable, a little more authentic, a little more real for a season in your Hummer, and then we'll eventually downsize you to a smaller car when you're ready."

This makes sense to my brain. It's a vulnerable transition, but it feels possible. I might get hit, but I would take less damage in a Hummer than on a bicycle. And it's a process that I can understand, one where I can walk a path of being more vulnerable and more open to connections and relationships. It's a step I can take, a step in the right direction.

I encourage you to begin some awareness around your coping mechanisms. If you find that you have some that aren't serving you anymore, maybe it's time to downsize.

Instead of isolation, you could try humor. Sometimes we all just need to laugh, and sometimes that laughter can help us be authentic about the places that need healing. Songs, stories, books, movies can also be very therapeutic. These things all allow us a way of talking about and engaging difficult places around shame. By identifying with a song or movie or story, it feels a little safer and a little bit more removed from us, and it allows us a chance to deal with some difficult pain in our life.

Layers of Shame

For many years I taught this material as part of a class at George Fox University. I used to do different exercises with it, and one of them was called "layers of shame". The day the students came in for the exercise, I would have them bring bedsheets. Then I would arrange the students in a circle, with someone sitting in the middle of the circle. The person sitting in the center was kind of our test subject, and they were there to represent the whole class. We would then begin to talk about places of shame. Sometimes the shame was about their personal lives, sometimes it was more theoretical. Each time someone would bring up a new shame illustration, I would have that person go lay a sheet on top of the person in the center of the room.

We would do that again and again and again until that one person had eight or nine or ten sheets over top of them, sort of representing the layers of separation and disconnect that shame causes in relationships.

After the sheets had been added, we would talk to the person who was in the center of the room, blanketed with all these layers of shame. They always said the same sorts of things: they felt it getting darker and darker as the layers piled on; they felt more and more cut off from the relationships in the room. But the funny thing is, they almost always said that, after a while, they got kind of comfortable under there. They were cut off, they were alone, it was dark ... but it was kind of okay. They were so disconnected that they stopped feeling the disconnect after a while. The layers became like a sort of coping mechanism.

But that wasn't the end of the exercise. After we had piled all the layers on, we began to remove them by talking about redeeming those moments of shame. We would read grace statements, and we would have people go forward, one by one, to take a layer off. Little by little, sort of like going from that tank down to that bike, the person under the layers of shame would find more and more freedom. They would hear more. They would see more. Finally, the last sheet would come off and they were back in the room with us. Then we could debrief how that experience felt as well.

The point is this, this process of reintegrating takes time. Every time I did that exercise, I would have at least one student who would say something like, "I wanted to go up and rip all of the sheets of shame off of the person when we got done with the shame statements. That disconnection and alienation felt so horrible, and I wanted to bring them back all at once so they could be with us again."

Every time somebody said that, do you know what the person underneath the sheets said? "I'm glad you didn't do that. I wasn't ready for 8 - 10 sheets to be taken off of me all at once. I had to kind of reintegrate enough to remember that there are other people in the room. I had to start hearing your voices, seeing the light come in. The weight lifted slowly, and that was a good thing. I wanted to go through the process, to experience each layer of healing."

I will always remember that. We have to appreciate the value of the process as we help ourselves and others find healing. It's a journey, and it takes time.

Empathy

Show me a person who struggles with shame, and I'll show you a person who has a hard time receiving empathy. It's a bold statement, but it's true. Now, it's probably also true that this person hasn't received much empathy in their lifetime, which is why they are trapped in their shame. But the flipside is also true... they probably have a hard time receiving empathy. Giving *and* receiving it, but especially receiving it.

They just kind of freeze when you try to show them care or empathy or appreciation. They don't know what to say. They don't know where to put empathy and care, because it's foreign to them. Somebody told me once that it's a little bit like having a rusted-out pail. People are trying to pour empathy and care and affirmation into it, but the pail doesn't have a bottom in it. It's all rusted out. The empathy has nowhere to go.

But here's the good news: working through shame and going through a process of healing starts to build a little bit of a grid in the bottom of the bucket. A little bit of a webbing starts to form, a process which eventually helps us learn how to hold some empathy. Sometimes it starts with just saying, "thank you". Verbalizing that in response to empathy helps build an ability to receive and hold empathy from people.

Receiving empathy is a vulnerable thing to do. It takes trust, real communication, and a quieting of the internal critic. Empathy is an art, and it's one we would do well to develop.

Empathy is when someone behaves as though they have walked a mile in your shoes, when they really understand what it is like to be *you*. I tell my students all the time when we are practicing empathy with clients: when you can mirror back the words and the feelings a client shares with you so perfectly that the response is."Yes, exactly!", you know you've got it.

Curt Thompson explains the power of empathy in his book, *Anatomy of the Soul*: "If, however, you encounter a therapist or a good friend who, when you feel sad, responds with empathy and comfort, your memory of the feeling of sadness will change, even if ever so little at first. You will also change your future because now that you have experienced a different reaction to your sadness, you can anticipate a different response."[43]

There is something so healing and empowering and validating about someone paying enough attention to you that they can

---

[43] Thompson, Curt. *Anatomy of the Soul: Surprising Connections between Neuroscience and Spiritual Practices That Can Transform Your Life and Relationships*. Carrollton, TX, Tyndale, 2010, p. 78.

repeat back to you not only your words and experience, but your feelings. When they can understand your head, your heart, and your hands. In those moments, you feel a connection that already begins a process of healing. You know someone is with you and for you. You have experienced the grace of empathy.

Shame Traps

As we build skills for shame resilience and learn to thrive in healing and grace, we must be especially aware of what Nancy Thurston calls "shame traps".[44] These are the situations where there is no way to win. It's a "damned if you do, damned if you don't" sort of place. You are between a rock and a hard place with someone, and no matter what path you take, you know you are not going to make everyone happy and that there will be an opportunity for shame to take root.

For years, I shared this information with students and said that someday, if I ever get famous – like if I write a book on shame or something – and I get on Oprah, or on Brené Brown's podcast, I was going to say: we've all had these

_____

[44] Thurston, Nancy. "When Perfect Fear Casts Out All Love." *Journal of Psychology and Christianity*, 13, 1994, pp. 69 – 75.

experiences where we can't win, and I'm going give you a little hint for what to do when you find yourself in a shame trap: *if you're damned if you do, and damned if you don't ... wait for it ... do whatever you damn well please!*

Excuse the glib language here, but sometimes we can just get way too hard on ourselves trying to please everyone or honor all sides of a situation. Sometimes, there is no way to win. Sometimes we have to make choices and live with consequences. Remember our spiritual foundation, where we talked about God helping us to move into maturity? This is part of that process. As we mature, we learn that we sometimes have to make decisions in life that will not make everybody happy.

Sometimes, we just have to make judgment calls with the best wisdom, clarity, compassion, and understanding we have.

The year 2020 brought on a whole onslaught of these double bind shame traps, didn't it? Think of all the impossible calls we had to make as quarantine lifted and we attempted to live life before a vaccine arrived. There was such an incredibly diverse array of opinions about mask wearing and social distancing and exposure timelines and event capacities. I'm willing to wager that in almost every extended family or church community in this country, not everyone was in complete agreement about how to handle holidays or reopenings or weddings or school or any of it. Any decision made to satisfy one side of the table would surely bring up some anger and accusation from the other side of it.

And do you know what resulted from all the anger and accusation? Shame. A whole lot of shame.

Now, I wouldn't use glib language to tell you how to handle a pandemic. It's been a life-changing, unprecedented challenge for all of us. But I would tell you this: if you are making a decision based on the wisdom, clarity, compassion, and understanding that you have, if you are holding to your own personal values and seeking the will of the Spirit to the best of your ability, then there is *no cause for shame*.

Power Defining Statements

Part of the process of getting healthier and developing resilience to shame is to acknowledge that other people's opinions don't have to define your life and reality. We must learn to say, as Nancy Thurston writes, "You are certainly entitled to your opinion of me, but I do not have to agree with your opinion of me."[45] This is a *power defining statement*.

---

[45] Thurston, Nancy. "When Perfect Fear Casts Out All Love." *Journal of Psychology and Christianity*, 13, 1994, pp. 69 – 75.

Other people are allowed to have thoughts and feelings about me, whether I like those thoughts and feelings or not. I might not be able to change their thoughts and feelings just by changing my words or behavior, but I do not have to agree with what they think of me. I do not have to receive the shame they are asking me to pick up. I do not have to adapt my behavior to suit their judgments. I am allowed to stand in my own power.

Let's try that statement again, and see how it flows for you:

"You are certainly entitled to your opinion of me, but I do not have to agree with your opinion of me."

By saying these words, we are putting some boundaries in place. We are not shaming them or invalidating them for their perspectives; we are simply refusing to pick up the shame they are consciously or sometimes unconsciously throwing at us.

Of course, this doesn't mean that people's perspectives are not valuable. On the contrary, it's essential to have help in moving material from our "blind box" to our "open box", as we learned about with the Johari model. My recommendation, however, is to be very selective with the people that you allow to speak into these places. Are their words coming from a place of compassion and a true desire to help you heal? Or are their words coming from a place of fear and judgment?

Do their words empower you to pursue further health, or discourage you to a deeper place of shame? Most often, words that cause shame are coming from a place of shame in the speaker. Don't allow people to speak brokenness into you out of their own brokenness.

A Prayer

I hope that these recommendations and processes will be helpful to you as you pursue a life of grace. But more than any scientific discovery or physiological mechanism, the guiding voice of your healing will always be the Spirit of Christ Jesus.

Let's pray.

Spirit of the Living God, the only thing we can say after that is, thank you. We are indebted to you, and we are thankful for what you have done on our behalf. Because of the work you have done for us and because of the commitment and the care and love and grace you show us, we are compelled to be people of grace in our world and in our relationships. Help us to do that as we receive the healing you so generously offer. In the name of Jesus we pray, Amen.

CONCLUSION

In full honesty and transparency, I spent many days thinking and praying about how exactly to end a book on shame and grace. What exhortation could I give you that would propel you towards change and healing? What expert could I quote that would say it all in finer words than mine? What scripture could I leave you with that would do its holy work in your heart?

Perhaps, however, we have had enough of exhortations and experts and even scriptures.

Perhaps, instead, I will leave you with a story.

In 1995, I was finishing up my doctoral work at Fuller Seminary in southern California. My wife Karen was pregnant at the time with our first child, Taylor, and we were all kinds of excited. About halfway through the pregnancy, we got the call offering me a job at Western Evangelical Seminary, which later became George Fox University. Our dreams and plans were coming together before our eyes!

After we made the move to the Portland metro area, we met with a new doctor for Karen and the baby. At our very first visit, they discovered some major concerns. Things were not developing properly with the baby, and they gave us the option of doing further testing or just letting the pregnancy continue.

We thought and talked and prayed about it, and since we have always tended to want more information rather than less, we opted to do the continued testing.

Our first child, Taylor Alexandria, was diagnosed with Trisomy 18. This rare condition meant that she had a 3rd 18th chromosome. Her lungs were not developed, her brain was not developed, her heart was not developed. Life expectancy was estimated at days or maybe weeks after birth, if she survived at all.

As we walked out of the doctor's office with all that information, we were faced with a decision of whether we were going to abort our first pregnancy or move forward with it. There was some concern for Karen's body if we were to go through with the pregnancy, and of course we were weighing all of the mental, emotional, and spiritual strain of a decision one way or the other. It's one thing to read about a scenario like this in the Bible or an ethics course, but it's another thing to drive home with your wife after being in that doctor's appointment, knowing that you have a huge decision to make.

We cried, we prayed, we talked with family and friends. We wanted to make a good decision, a decision that made sense and was right in the eyes of God. As you know, I was raised as a very conservative Christian, and the morality of the decision was extremely important to both Karen and me.

Our whole family and everyone around us was devastated. My dad was going through his ordination process at the time, and he happened to be in the middle of an ethics course, which he ended up delaying because of the grief and trauma to all of us. I remember my dad calling me as we were in the process of making the decision and telling me that he had had a dream that we went forward with the birth, and both Karen and the baby died during childbirth. He felt like the reason we went forward was because of him, because of how he raised us. He was afraid that because of him, they would both die. After that dream, my dad told me this: *whatever you decide, I have your back, 100%. Your mother and I will be with you in support all the way, no matter what.*

That moment was the most grace-filled moment I can ever remember experiencing from my parents.

My parents chose to engage us with love and grace and acceptance, no matter what. Somehow, that release of pressure and expectation was enough to allow Karen and I to make the choice that we felt was right, that would be the least long-term emotionally scarring experience. We went ahead with the pregnancy.

Taylor was born and died in late 1995. It was an incredibly

difficult time for our family. We went back to Nebraska and had a funeral for Taylor, and the grace of our families as we grieved was more healing than I could ever express.

Eventually, life moved on. My dad went back to finish his ordination work. We ended up having 2 more children, Madison and Parker, 2 and 4 years later.

Years later, I ran into a man who had been the professor of my dad's ethics course while we were going through the loss of Taylor. He recognized my name and told me that he knew my dad. He remembered my dad wrestling with all this during the ethics course, remembering him needing to leave the course so that he could be free to choose grace for his son. He spoke of my dad's love for me and his own respect in what my dad chose to do.

Taylor's life matters. My prayer is that by hearing her story, perhaps you will feel invited and encouraged to give or receive grace. This is the way of Jesus, and it heals brokenness of every kind.

I hope what comes through in this story, more than anything, is that *a grace experience taught me more than anything I read or researched about grace.*

I know this is a heavy story. I am literally praying as I write it, because I want you to hear the transformational beauty that is woven into these threads of grace. I hope that what you see and hear in this story is that my parents, conservative Christians who loved Jesus and valued their understanding of Biblical doctrine, chose *relationships*, their children, over denominational *doctrine*. Our entire family was faced with the most personal life and death dilemma ever. With God's help, we came closer to one another, not further away.

Grace chooses relationship every time.

My parents have since passed away. I have no doubt that they are part of the cloud of witnesses, alongside of Taylor, in heaven. Even to this day, I can hardly articulate what their decision of grace means to me. It was real. It was authentic. It was felt. It was lived. It changed me. That is what GRACE does. It changes you.

I hope that something shared in this book helps you in your journey of living with Shame No More! I hope that your broken places find restoration and that your relationships experience healing. More than anything, my prayer as we end this journey together is that *you are changed by God's grace ... and that you change others with God's grace.*

May it be so.

APPENDIX

For Professionals

This appendix is specifically written to leaders, pastors, professional counselors, mental health coaches, and other professionals who care for the hearts of people. God gives us grace so that we can become someone that gives grace away to somebody else. Your chosen work reflects the love and grace of God Himself, and I am grateful for your efforts. Perhaps these suggestions can be helpful and useful to you in some way.

Recommendations for Therapists, Leaders, and Relationship Coaches:

•   View people with unconditional positive regard. See in others the potential to be healed through God's grace. Everyone has potential because they are made in the image of God. Learn to treat everyone like this and see possibility and hope, even if you can't see it in the present moment.

•   Maintain your significant values and spiritual beliefs without becoming judgmental or imposing them. Believe what you believe, but don't write those beliefs in stone. Be in process. Learn. Grow. And make room for people to be different from you, without judging them.

•	Acknowledge, learn about, and develop empathy for the distinct needs of people, especially around grace and shame. Empathy is the key to connecting deeply with people different than you. Practice it. Make room to be with and honor those different than you. Make effort to validate and understand people different than you.

•	Accept and love people where they are, and encourage them toward growth, change, and a grace-filled journey. Remember, we are all in process. We are all changing and growing. Accept people today and know that they may change tomorrow!

•	Build a base of general knowledge about how spirituality and religious traditions impact our lives, and keep learning. Spirituality is the key element in all our lives that makes the difference. Invest time to read about and understand different belief systems from your own. Use your understanding to connect with others, and meet them where they are.

•	Become dispensers of God's grace and representatives of his love to bring people into freedom, self-acceptance, and relationship with him. Witness. Witness with your life, and maybe with your words.

Recommendations for Pastors, Priests, and Christian Lay Counselors:

• See altar calls and church gatherings as ways to hear from and talk with a relational God, not as tools to shame people into heaven. Make prayer, both in public and private, into a holy moment of place and time to connect with a loving God. Be aware of anything that sounds like a fear-based "get-out-of-hell" card.

• Make it a goal for church meetings and special services to inspire grace for a stable and ongoing relationship with God. Avoid adrenaline-based experiences. While summer camp or mountain-top experiences with God are great, the goal is the overall trajectory of relationship. Over the long haul, lead your people toward the ever upward journey, with ups and downs, peaks and valleys.

• Present prayer as natural communication between people and their loving Father to build mutually desired intimacy. Pray always. As you live life, be inviting God into your daily life, like you do your best friend.

• Accept sin as human and forgivable so that people can experience holiness based on relationship, not behavior. We are all sinful creatures in process. But we also are maturing and growing in relationship with others and with our God. Holiness is being with God, daily, in all of life.

•   Build a community of faith that uplifts, supports and loves the wounded and spiritually dying back to health. I imagine you have heard that churches are supposed to be more like hospitals then country clubs. Churches are communities. Places where we grow alongside others caring, loving, supporting, and holding each other accountable for how we are in the world.

•   Become dispensers of God's grace and representatives of his love to bring people into freedom, self-acceptance, and relationship to him. Witness. Life will provide you the opportunities to walk out grace daily in relationship with everyone around you. Like the shoe giant says: Just Do It.

Dr. Shaw's Must-Reads:

People often ask me for recommended reading, and of course I have dozens of books to recommend on the subjects covered in this book! But here is a list of the books that have been most influential for my understanding of shame and grace and healing. Perhaps they will be helpful to you, too. Happy Reading!

•   Jack and Judy Balswick, *The Family*

•   Claudia Black, *Changing Course: Healing from Loss,*

Abandonment and Fear

- Everything from Brené Brown!

- Kurt Bubna, *Epic Grace*

- Dearing and Tangney, *Shame in the Therapy Hour*

- Terry Hargrave, *Restoration Therapy*

- Helmeke & Sori, *The Therapist's Notebook for Integrating Spirituality in Counseling* (Someone has a chapter in this book...hmmm)

- Mark McMinn, *Sin and Grace in Christian counseling*

- Eugene Peterson, *The Message*

- David Seamands, *Healing Grace*

- Lewis Smedes, *Shame and Grace*

- Steve Stephens, *Marriage: Experience the Best*

- Curt Thompson, *The Soul of Shame* and *Anatomy of the Soul*

- Paul Tournier, *The Meaning of Persons*

- Mary Stewart Van Leeuwen, *Gender and Grace*

- Jeff VanVonderen, *Tired of Trying to Measure Up*

ACKNOWLEDGEMENTS

So many people played significant roles in bringing this work to completion. Thank you all! I could not have done it without each of you! If you read this and think it might be you...it is!

To every family member, friend, professor, fellow student, colleague, client, supervisor, pastor,& mentor: thank you for the attention, opportunity, wisdom, and grace you poured into me.

Jay, thank you. Without O Grill & you, this book would have never made it to print.

Naponee Wesleyan Church, thank you for being a place of grace to me.

Shame & Grace Graduate students at George Fox University, Portland, OR., thank you! Your zeal, questions, feedback, papers, and authentic personal and professional processes every time I taught the course inspired me to believe that maybe someone outside of us might just be impacted by this material.

David, thank you for introducing me to the language of Shame and Grace as a way to organize thoughts, feelings, behaviors, experiences, and relationships.

Lewis, thank you for teaching me that there are many ways to accomplish the same outcome.

Jack & Judy, thank you for believing in me and helping me to do this work professionally.

Les, thank you for living out the application of grace to me.

Fred & Larry, thank you for giving me the chance to be in the field professionally.

Willamette Valley Wesleyan, SouthLake, & Evergreen Foursquare Churches, thank you for giving me so many opportunities to teach, preach, and practice this material.

Melody, thank you for hours and hours of work you did that, quite frankly, I had tried to do myself and was unable to complete.

Dearest, Star, Sunshine, Moonbeam, Rev & Mrs. Rev, thank you for practicing grace with me, even though I am a slow learner.

COMING SOON

Be sure to watch for Dr. Shaw's next book, *Shame No More - The Study Guide,* coming early 2022.

Visit ShameNoMore.com or Amazon for more details.

CPSIA information can be obtained
at www.ICGtesting.com
Printed in the USA
FSHW012037240122
87889FS